High School Lesson Plans Teachers Can Actually Use!

Language Arts

by

JJ Botta

Copyright

ISBN: 978-0-578-06962-3

R©

Roost Publications, LLC

Dedication

This book is dedicated to high school teachers everywhere. Until I joined your ranks, I never realized how hard you work, and how you influence the lives of your students. Thank you.

Table of Contents

Preface

High School Lesson Plans Teachers Can Actually Use! is a practical collection of language arts lesson plans English teachers have long awaited. In the age of government standards, district regulations, and school board requirements, lesson plans available to teachers have become complicated and impractical, and often require materials not readily accessible to the classroom professional. The plans in this book are easy to follow, extremely effective, and require no additional materials to implement. These lesson plans may be used by the high school teacher for spontaneous class assignments, as supplements to regular language arts themes, or for use by substitute teachers – with ease!

Author's Note

As of the printing of this book, every state in the union has adopted some degree of standards for their individual language arts programs for high school students. It is virtually impossible for any author to include into a single volume lesson plans specifically earmarked for compliance with the idiosyncrasies of educators compiling each state standard. Additionally, the language arts standards in every state, while substantially the same, are continually in flux from jurisdiction to jurisdiction in the United States. Therefore, my approach has been from the opposite direction. I have attempted to investigate the various standards approved by individual state jurisdictions, identify commonalities, and strive not to violate any of them. I hope that I have accomplished my task. I do stress to individual teachers, however, that from year to year prudence dictates checking state standards prior to utilizing any lesson plans in the classroom.

Over the last decade, most state boards of education have collaborated to develop a uniform and specific vision of what students should know and be able to do in the subject area of language arts. The consensus among educators is primarily to establish high expectations for all students, enabling them to pursue their own goals and interests throughout their lives. At every grade level, the standards cover reading, writing, written and oral English language conventions, and listening and speaking is encompassed in all state standard revisions each year. Reading, writing, listening, and speaking are related processes, which should be nurtured within a rich core curriculum in every state in order for students to achieve knowledge across the disciplines. Literacy is inextricably linked to knowledge. It must be remembered that the standards in every state must demonstrate *what* to teach, not *how* to teach. Teachers must mold lesson plans to fit both their best teaching styles and the needs of their children.

jjb

High School Lesson Plans Teachers Can Actually Use!

Language Arts

Poetry

Metaphors & Similes

Objective: To demonstrate to students how to locate and interpret the poetic devices of *metaphor* and *simile* to help them understand the meanings of poems.

Step 1 – Warm-up: Ask students to think about the concept of love. Then, have them write a short poem comparing their interpretation of love to people, places, objects, or experiences of their choosing. When they have finished writing their poetry, select several students to read their poems aloud to the class, and have the class briefly comment and discuss them.

Step 2 – Introduction to the Lesson: Following the warm-up, explain the following literary elements to the class:

figurative language is language expanded beyond its *literal* meanings. Two examples are *metaphors* and *similes*. The purpose of such language is to create imagery in the minds of the readers, which helps interpret the poet's meaning.

metaphor: a direct comparison between two unlike things that does not use the words *like* or *as.*

simile: a comparison of two unlike things using the words *like* or *as.*

Step 3 – Activity: Select a poem of the teacher's choice containing similes and metaphors. A good selection would be *Mirror* by Sylvia Plath, which can easily be found in poetry selections or online. Since numerous poems contain similes and metaphors, it is very easy for the teacher to select the poetry of his or her choice for this assignment. Simply write the poem of choice on the classroom whiteboard for all to read.

Be certain students read the poem the first time for enjoyment only. On their second reading, have them make note of any metaphors or similes used by the poet. After identifying the figurative language, ask them to write a short essay on how the meaning of the poem is made clearer by focusing on the metaphors and similes found.

Teacher's Note: The poem *Mirror* is an excellent choice because it is open widely to interpretation. The mirror is a reflection of the reader's individual personality (and perhaps the poet's, as well).

Step 4 – Discussion: When the class has completed the essays, select several students to read their essays aloud, and discuss them openly. Be certain to point out any figurative language used, especially metaphors and similes, and relate their use to the overall meaning of the poems written.

Step 5 – Assessment: As a homework assignment, have the students select a poem of their choice, and tell them to be prepared to

read the selected poems aloud in class.
Students should be able to point out the
figurative language in the poems they choose,
especially metaphors and similes, and explain
how they help readers understand the meaning
of each poem.

Alliteration

Objective: To demonstrate to students how the poetic device of *alliteration* helps the reader focus on images the poet creates, which better enables readers to understand the meanings of poems.

Step 1 – Warm-up: Ask students to write a short poem on any subject they choose. Tell them they must attempt to repeat the first letters at the beginning of several words in their poems. For example, "**S**he **s**ells **s**ea **s**hells by the **s**ea **s**hore." When they have finished writing their poetry, select several students to read their poems aloud to the class, and have the class briefly comment and discuss them.

Step 2 – Introduction to the Lesson: Following the warm-up, explain the nature of the literary element of *alliteration* to the class:

      alliteration is the repetition of sounds at the beginnings of words. The purpose of this poetic device is to focus the attention of readers on images and moods the poet intends to create. Identification of these parts of a poem particularly important to the poet helps readers to interpret the poet's meaning.

Step 3 – Activity: *The Rime of the Ancient Mariner* by Samuel Taylor Coleridge is a famous lengthy poem that tells the story of a long sea journey, where a ship is driven off course by a storm. Ask students to read the following two stanzas from the poem, which are taken from different sections of Part Two of the work. The poet creates different scenes for the reader using the technique of alliteration:

excerpt #1

The fair breeze blew, the white foam flew,
The furrow followed free ;
We were the first that ever burst
Into that silent sea.

excerpt #2

Water, water, every where,
And all the boards did shrink ;
Water, water, every where,
Nor any drop to drink.
In me she has drowned a young girl, and in me
an old woman
Rises toward her day after day, like a terrible
fish.

Be certain students read the poem the first time
for enjoyment only. On their second reading,
have them make note of any use of alliteration
by the poet. After identifying alliteration, ask
them to write a short essay on how the
meaning of the poem is made clearer by
focusing on the images and moods discovered
through the alliteration found in the poem.

Teacher's Note: This poem is an excellent
choice because it is riddled with alliteration.
Students will easily identify the repetition of
sounds, forcing them to focus on Coleridge's
imagery.

Step 4 – Discussion: When the class has completed the essays, select several students to read their essays aloud, and discuss them openly. Be certain to point out the alliteration used, and the resulting mood and imagery, and relate the use of repetitive sounds to the overall ease of understanding the meaning of the poems written.

Step 5 – Assessment: As a homework assignment, have the students select other sections or stanzas from the poem, *"The Rime of the Ancient Mariner,"* and tell them to be prepared to read their selections aloud in class. Students should be able to point out the use of alliteration in the stanzas they choose, and explain how it helps to explain the meaning of each stanza.

Free Verse

Objective: To demonstrate to students that the concept of *free verse* in poetry does not mean a lack of poetic characteristics.

Step 1 – Warm-up: Ask students to think about their understanding of the concept of poetic *free verse*. Then, have them write a short poem about people, places, objects, or experiences of their choosing using *their* understanding of *free verse*. When they have finished writing their poetry, select several students to read their poems aloud to the class, and have the class briefly comment and discuss them.

Step 2 – Introduction to the Lesson: Following the warm-up, explain the following literary element to the class:

> **free verse:** poetry written without a regular rhyme scheme, meter, or form, but

based on its complexities is still recognizable as poetry.

Step 3 – Activity: Ask students to read the following poem:

from *Song of Myself*

I CELEBRATE myself, and sing myself,
And what I assume you shall assume,
For every atom belonging to me as good belongs to you.

I loafe and invite my soul,
I lean and loafe at my ease observing a spear of summer grass.

My tongue, every atom of my blood, form'd from this soil, this air,
Born here of parents born here from parents the same, and their
parents the same,
I, now thirty-seven years old in perfect health

begin,
Hoping to cease not till death.

Creeds and schools in abeyance,
Retiring back a while sufficed at what they are,
but never forgotten,
I harbor for good or bad, I permit to speak at
every hazard,
Nature without check with original energy.

by Walt Whitman

Be certain students read the poem the first time
for enjoyment only. On their second reading,
have them make note of any poetic devices or
figurative language used by the poet. Then, ask
them to write two short poems on their own
lives, one using traditional poetic form,
including rhyme and meter, and one using free
verse.

Teacher's Note: This poem is an excellent
choice because it is about the poet's own
reflections on his life. Students will find it easy

to write about events in their own lives, but will quickly recognize that free verse is not *easier* to write than traditional poetic forms, only different.

Step 4 – Discussion: When the class has completed the poems, select several students to read their poems aloud, and discuss them openly. Be certain to point out any figurative language used in their free verse versions, and discuss the effectiveness of the poems written in both styles.

Step 5 – Assessment: As a homework assignment, have the students write a brief essay on the differences and similarities between free verse and traditional poetic forms.

Reading a Poem

Objective: To help students through the form of a *sonnet* discover several ways to read a poem, which enables readers to understand the meanings of poems and the forms and poetic devices used by the poet.

Step 1 – Warm-up: Ask students to write a one stanza, fourteen-line poem on any subject they choose. Tell them they must give the poem a title, use rhymes, use repeated words, and pay special attention to the first and last lines of their poems. When they have finished writing their poetry, select several students to read their poems aloud to the class, and have the class briefly comment and discuss them.

Step 2 – Introduction to the Lesson: Following the warm-up, explain the following to the class:

Reading a Poem requires a degree of skill. To understand the meaning of a poem clearly, readers should set a *purpose* for reading the poem selected. By focusing on simple concepts like the title, rhyme schemes, repetition, and the first and last lines of a poem, readers discover a considerable amount of information making it easier to comprehend the poet's message.

Italian (Petrarchan) Sonnet: A fourteen-line poem with a rhyme scheme that has two parts – the *octave* (an eight-line scheme) and the *sestet* (a six-line scheme). In the poem that follows, the octave has a rhyme scheme of ABBAABBA, and the sestet has a rhyme scheme of CDECDE.

Step 3 – Activity: *How do I love thee? Let me count the ways* by Elizabeth Barrett Browning is a classic love poem. Ask students to read the Browning poem, noting (in writing) the title, rhyme schemes, repetition, the first and last lines of the poem, and any other literary devices they recognize:

How do I love thee? Let me count the ways

by Elizabeth Barrett Browning

How do I love thee? Let me count the ways.
I love thee to the depth and breadth and height
My soul can reach, when feeling out of sight
For the ends of Being and ideal Grace.
I love thee to the level of everyday's
Most quiet need, by sun and candle-light.
I love thee freely, as men strive for Right;
I love thee purely, as they turn from Praisc.
I love thee with a passion put to use
In my old griefs, and with my childhood's faith.
I love thee with a love I seemed to lose
With my lost saints, --- I love thee with the
breath,
Smiles, tears, of all my life! --- and, if God
choose,
I shall but love thee better after death.

Be certain students read the poem the first time
for enjoyment only. On their second reading,

have them make note of the sonnet form (ABBAABBA CDECDE). Students should highlight repeated words and rhyming words. They should attempt to derive the meaning of the poem by examining its title, and the first and last lines.

Teacher's Note: This poem is an excellent choice because it is an obvious love poem. The specifics of the nature of the speaker's love are easily found in the poetic devices the students are being asked to highlight.

Step 4 – Discussion: When the class has read the Browning selection and completed its notations, have several of the class members discuss the similarities and differences between Browning's poem and the poetry they wrote during the warm-up exercise. They should be specific, relating the poetic devices used to the overall ease of understanding the meaning of the poems written.

Step 5 – Assessment: As a homework assignment, have the students select two poems with different poetic rhyme schemes, such as *villanelles, odes,* or *quatrains.* They should be prepared to explain to the class how reading the selected poem with a purpose, more specifically, looking for rhyme schemes, examining the titles, checking for alliteration, and focusing on the first and last lines of each poem, help the reader extract the poet's meaning from each work.

Poetry & Music

Objective: To help students explore some of the similarities and differences between poetry and modern music.

Step 1 – Warm-up: Ask students to write the lyrics to their favorite popular song. Tell them they can use lyrics from an existing song, but if they would prefer, they are free to write a song of their own. They should also write down the title of the song. When they have finished writing their songs, select several students to read (or sing) their popular song or creation aloud to the class, and have the class briefly comment and discuss them.

Step 2 – Introduction to the Lesson: Following the warm-up, explain the following to the class:

   rhyme is the repetition of words that have the same ending sound.

rhyme scheme is the pattern of end rhyme in a poem.

rhythm is the musical quality created by a pattern of stressed and unstressed syllables.

meter is the basic rhythmic structure of a verse in poetry. Meter in poetry is like the *beat* in music.

refrain is a phrase or verse that is repeated at the end of each of the separate stanzas of a poetic composition.

Explain to the class that contemporary songs are accompanied by voices and instruments, adding effects that written poetry lacks. Modern songs are usually divided into five sections:

a. An instrumental or verbal introduction.

b. The first verse, followed by a refrain.

c. The second verse, followed by a refrain.

d. A verse that changes the melody, rhyme, or pattern of the first two verses (very often a solo verse by the lead singer).

e. The fourth verse (with the same rhythmical pattern as the first two verses), followed by a refrain.

Step 3 – Activity: Ask students to read the following famous poem:

Song: To Celia

Drink to me only with thine eyes,
　And I will pledge with mine;
Or leave a kiss but in the cup,
　And I'll not look for wine.
The thirst that from the soul doth rise
　Doth ask a drink divine;

But might I of Jove's nectar sup,
  I would not change for thine.

I sent thee late a rosy wreath,
  Not so much honouring thee
As giving it a hope, that there
  It could not withered be.
But thou thereon didst only breathe,
  And sent'st it back to me;
Since when it grows, and smells, I swear,
  Not of itself, but thee.

by Ben Johnson

Be certain students read the poem the first time for enjoyment only. On their second reading, have them make note of any rhyme, rhyme scheme, rhythm, meter, or refrain.

Teacher's Note: This poem is an excellent choice because, although it is a famous poem, it is an obvious song. Students will find it easy to compare to modern popular musical selections.

Step 4 – Discussion: When the class has read the Johnson poem and completed its notations, have several of the class members discuss the similarities and differences between *Song: To Celia* and the song they wrote during the warm-up exercise. They should be specific, referring to the rhyme, rhyme scheme, rhythm, meter, and refrain, if any, in each. Students should be able to discuss the effects each of these elements have upon the meaning intended to be conveyed by the poet or songwriter.

Step 5 – Assessment: As a homework assignment, have the students write down the lyrics to two of their favorite popular songs. They should be prepared to explain to the class the poetic qualities contained in the lyrics selected, with a focus on rhyme, rhyme scheme, rhythm, meter, and refrain.

Self-Expression

Objective: To demonstrate to students how poetry is a form of self-expression used by poets to tell others about personal experiences that have affected their lives.

Step 1 – Warm-up: Ask students to create a timeline of events that have taken place in their lives. Direct them to write brief descriptions next to each event in their timelines, including the date each took place and the location of each event. When they have finished writing their timelines, select several students to read their experiences aloud to the class, and have the class briefly comment and discuss them.

Step 2 – Introduction to the Lesson: Following the warm-up, explain the following to the class:

All human beings experience changes in their lives. Change might be significant or subtle, gratifying or unsatisfying, good or bad.

The changes we experience cause us to discover new concepts, and often compel us to make decisions that affect, or even alter, our lives. Poets draw from their memories the events and effects that have impressed them in their lives, and relate those events to us through an expression of their feelings.

Step 3 – Activity: Ask students to read the following poem:

I heard a Fly buzz -- when I died

I heard a Fly buzz -- when I died --
The Stillness in the Room
Was like the Stillness in the Air --
Between the Heaves of Storm --

The Eyes around -- had wrung them dry --
And Breaths were gathering firm
For that last Onset -- when the King
Be witnessed -- in the Room --

I willed my Keepsakes -- Signed away

What portion of me be
Assignable -- and then it was
There interposed a Fly --

With Blue -- uncertain stumbling Buzz --
Between the light -- and me --
And then the Windows failed -- and then
I could not see to see --

      by Emily Dickinson

Be certain students read the poem the first time
for enjoyment only. On their second reading,
have them make notc of the speaker's
experiences and the *feelings* associated with
them.

Teacher's Note: This poem deals with
Dickinson's obsession with death. It begins
with the speaker hearing a fly buzzing by as she
is dying. The stanzas that follow set the scene
of the death experience. Note the "stillness in
the air," the preparations made by the
mourners for the speaker's passing, and the
presence of God, "the King be witnessed in the

room." Finally, the speaker envisions herself giving away her earthly possessions, as her life begins to fade away at the same time the buzzing of the fly diminishes. Students can readily understand these powerful emotions.

Step 4 – Discussion: When the class has completed its notations on the experiences and feelings expressed in the Dickinson poem, discuss them openly. Be certain to point out any figurative language used, and relate their use to the overall meaning of the poems written.

Step 5 – Assessment: As a homework assignment, have the students write a poem expressing their feelings and emotions about an experience that takes place in the *future*, and tell them to be prepared to read the selected poems aloud in class. Students should be able to point out how this future experience alters their lives, and discuss what life decisions they will be compelled to make as a result.

Writing About Our Surroundings

Objective: To demonstrate to students how poets draw their inspiration from their surroundings. Understanding this concept will help students better understand the meaning of poems.

Step 1 – Warm-up: Ask students to contemplate the world around them. Perhaps students have recently traveled to a foreign land, visited a national park or a major city. Perhaps they have simply dreamed of exotic places to one day explore. Ask students to prepare a short travel log of places they have seen or wish to see someday. Ask them to include both the positive and negative aspects of their experiences. When they have finished writing their travel logs, select several students to read them aloud to the class, and have the class briefly comment and discuss them.

Step 2 – Introduction to the Lesson:
Following the warm-up, explain the following literary elements to the class:

personification is a figure of speech in which poets give an animal, object, or idea human qualities, such as the ability to love, sing, cry, feel, talk, and make decisions.

figurative language is language expanded beyond its usual literal meanings. Metaphors and similes are two examples of the literary element of figurative language.

A **metaphor** is a direct comparison between two unlike things. It does not use the words *like* or *as*.

A **simile** compares two unlike things using the words *like* or *as*.

Explain to the class that literary elements are used by poets to create mental images for readers, helping readers to understand the meanings of their poems.

Step 3 – Activity: Ask students to read the following poem:

The Daffodils

I wander'd lonely as a cloud
That floats on high o'er vales and hills,
 all at once I saw a crowd,
A host, of golden daffodils;
Beside the lake, beneath the trees,
Fluttering and dancing in the breeze.

Continuous as the stars that shine
And twinkle on the Milky Way,
They stretch'd in never-ending line
Along the margin of a bay:
Ten thousand saw I at a glance,
Tossing their heads in sprightly dance.

The waves beside them danced; but they
Out-did the sparkling waves in glee:

A poet could not but be gay,
In such a jocund company:
I gazed -- and gazed -- but little thought
What wealth the show to me had
brought:

For oft, when on my couch I lie
In vacant or in pensive mood,
They flash upon that inward eye
Which is the bliss of solitude;
And then my heart with pleasure fills,
And dances with the daffodils.

by William Wordsworth

Be certain students read the poem the first time
for enjoyment only. On their second reading,
have them make note of any metaphors or
similes used by the poet. Have them pay
particular attention to the use of
personification. After identifying the figurative
language, ask them to write a short essay on
how the meaning of the poem is made clearer
by focusing on the literary elements identified.

Be certain they describe the *images* Wordsworth creates.

Teacher's Note: This poem is an excellent choice because Wordsworth uses personification quite effectively. He describes the daffodils and the waves as *dancing*, thereby bringing nature to life in a manner readers can easily envision.

Step 4 – Discussion: When the class has completed the essays, select several students to read their essays aloud, and discuss them openly. Be certain to point out any figurative language used, especially personification, and relate the use of this technique to the overall meaning of the poem. Be sure to discuss the possibilities of using personification in a poem created from the student travel logs prepared in the warm-up.

Step 5 – Assessment: As a homework assignment, have the students write a poem from the information described in their travel logs prepared in the warm-up exercise, and tell them to be prepared to read the selected poems aloud in class. Students should be able to point out the figurative language in the poems they choose, especially personification, metaphors, and similes, and explain how they help readers understand the images the poem creates.

What is Poetry?

Objective: Students will brainstorm definitions of poetry, expand their ideas as to the nature of poetry, and develop a working definition of poetry.

Step 1 – Warm-up: Ask students to define poetry. As the students call out their respective definitions, write them on the whiteboard. When they have finished brainstorming their ideas, have the class briefly comment and discuss each of them. Develop a working definition of poetry with which the class feels comfortable.

Step 2 – Introduction to the Lesson: Following the warm-up, explain the following accepted definitions of *poetry* to the class:

poetry is composed of carefully chosen words expressing great depth of meaning. This form of writing uses specific literary devices such as figurative language, sound, meter, and rhythm to express a combination of meaning and emotion.

traditional poetry follows a regular rhythmic pattern and rhyme scheme, and adheres to standard rules of grammar and syntax.

contemporary poetry is not bound by rhyme schemes or grammatical rules, but instead seeks new and unique methods of expression.

Step 3 – Activity: Begin with an open discussion comparing the collective definition of poetry developed during the warm-up session with the standard definitions listed in Step 2 above. Write the Margaret Walker poem, *I Want to Write*, on the whiteboard. After the class has formulated an understanding of the characteristics of poetry as a writing form, ask *three* student volunteers to read separately in turn the following poem aloud to the class:

I Want to Write

I want to write
I want to write the songs of my people.
I want to hear them singing melodies in the
dark.
I want to catch the last floating strains from
their sob-torn throats.
I want to frame their dreams into words; their
souls into notes.
I want to catch their sunshine laughter in a
bowl;
    fling dark hands to a darker sky
    and fill them full of stars
    then crush and mix such lights till they
become
    a mirrored pool of brilliance in the dawn.
               by Margaret Walker

Be certain the three reading students read the
poem slowly, with voice inflection. Have the
class make written notes of any poetic qualities
they recognize during the readings.

Teacher's Note: This poem by a 20th century African-American author addresses a myriad of easily recognizable common themes of freedom and hope, which students will relate to a variety of situations. Some frequent responses from students deal with the plight of Native Americans, as well as their own personal goals for the future.

Step 4 – Discussion: When the class has completed the readings of the poem, *I Want to Write,* have the students engage in a discussion as to whether or not the poem conforms to their definition of poetry, as well as the accepted definitions. Discuss any differences.

Step 5 – Assessment: Following the class discussion, have the students write two poems on a subject of their choice – one in a traditional format and one in a contemporary format. Tell them to write both poems *on the same subject matter.* Their poems will allow the teacher to assess their understanding as to the nature of poetry and the students' comfort level with a working definition of the poetic art form.

Poetry Links

Objective: This exercise is designed to tap the right side of a student's brain, allowing students to think as poets think. Students learn to trust their unconscious minds to create ideas that generate poetry. Even the most skeptical students will relax and develop the confidence needed to write poetry to express their inner feelings.

Step 1 – Warm-up: In this exercise, students are given an opportunity to daydream. Begin by telling the class they might or might not create a poem, but the warm-up is simply a chance to see what develops from the hidden thoughts in their minds. Assure them their creations will be neither graded nor criticized. It is just practice poetry to develop individual creativity. There will be no dictionaries, grammar or spelling requirements, or rhyming necessities, but merely a free association of words. They are not to consider their work a final product, but a rough, rough draft.

After introducing the warm-up, write a word such as *bus, home,* or *child* at the top of the whiteboard. Ask the students to write the same word at the top of their papers or writing journals. Then, ask someone in the class to suggest the first word that comes to his or her mind. For example, if the word chosen is *bus,* the student might suggest the word *travel.* Write the second word directly under the first word on the whiteboard. Then, ask another student what word the second word brings to mind. For example, the student might respond that *travel* makes her think of *vacation.* Continue this process until you (and the students on their papers) have written eight to ten words.

The teacher participates in this warm-up with the class. When the word list is complete, instruct the class to write a poem based on the word list, where each line in succession will contain the words on the word list. The students are told to write the first sentence that comes to mind with each selected word, regardless of how silly or disconnected they might seem. While the class is writing the poetry, the teacher is engaging in the same activity on the whiteboard. For example, my poem might turn out like this:

> Today I took a long *bus* ride,
> And it proved no way to take a *vacation*.
> Vacations should *relax* the mind and
body.
> Vacations should *refresh* the spirit.

> *Energy* must flow to get the mind to
grow,
> I can't return to my world *tired*.
> I saw how my father *labored* toward no
end.
> I understand what it means to be one
with *nature*.

> How awful it must be to *struggle*
unnecessarily with life,
> Which is not the path to *peace*.

When the poem is complete, read the finished draft to the class, and ask the students to compare how their poems developed similarly to or differently from your poem. Point out how the original idea of *bus* is drastically different from the finished idea of *peace*. Explain that this is because the hidden ideas in the mind are tapped subconsciously when we set our minds and thoughts free. Open the discussion to the class to exchange the collective thoughts of the students on the process of developing poetry in this manner.

Step 2 – Introduction to the Lesson:
Following the warm-up, explain the following accepted definitions of *poetry* to the class:

poetry is composed of carefully chosen words expressing great depth of meaning. This form of writing uses specific literary devices such as figurative language, sound, meter, and rhythm to express a combination of meaning and emotion.

traditional poetry follows a regular rhythmic pattern and rhyme scheme, and adheres to standard rules of grammar and syntax.

contemporary poetry is not bound by rhyme schemes or grammatical rules, but instead seeks new and unique methods of expression.

Step 3 – Activity: Ask each student to begin by selecting a word of his or her choice, and creating a word list for writing poetry in the same way the list was developed during the warm-up session in Step 1 above. Tell the class to begin writing poetry from the completed word list. Remind them to set their minds free by writing the first thoughts that enter their minds with each successive word.

Teacher's Note: We are told by Robert Frost that "A poem begins in delight and ends in wisdom." This exercise verifies Frost's impression. Even the students that are usually the most disinterested will actively participate in this activity. Since there are no specific rules, students are not quick to conclude that *poetry is boring* or they *are not good at it.*

Step 4 – Discussion: After the class has completed its poetry, ask for student volunteers to read their poetry aloud to the class. Allow for plenty of discussion on the resultant poems, their possible meanings, and the thought patterns generated.

Step 5 – Assessment: As a homework assignment, have the students write two poems in the same manner as they did in class. Tell them to be certain to produce a word list *prior* to the writing of their poems. They should be prepared to discuss both their word lists and their poetry drafts in the next class. Teachers will be able to recognize how the comfort level of the class with respect to writing poetry has improved. In addition, teachers will see that students performing this exercise learn how poets generate their ideas freely, without pressure. We are all poets.

The Diamante Poem

Objective: To demonstrate to students how the shape of poetry can often help them write poetry, as well as understand the meanings of poems.

Step 1 – Warm-up: Ask students to think about two, simple, diametrically opposed concepts, such as love and hate, or two opposite ideas or things, such as cats and dogs. Then, have the students write a short poem comparing the concepts, people, places, objects, or experiences they have chosen. When they have finished writing their poetry, select several students to read their poems aloud to the class, and have the class briefly comment and discuss them.

Step 2 – Introduction to the Lesson:
Following the warm-up, explain the concept of the *diamante* poem to the class:

    In French, the word *diamont* means diamond.

A **diamante** is a seven-line poem that gradually changes from one idea to a direct opposite idea. When the poem is completed, it is diamond-shaped. For example:

cat

scratch, cuddly

friendly, funny, warm

fluffy, meow, companion, pet

strong, shedding, loyal

fleas, bark

dog

Point out to the class how the first line contains one word, the second line two words, the third line three words, and the fourth line four words. Notice how the last two words of the fourth line begin to lead the changing of the concept from cat to dog. Line five contains three words, line six contains two words, and line seven contains one word. Lines one and seven are *opposite* concepts.

Step 3 – Activity: Ask students to begin with the contrasting concepts they used to write the warm-up poems, but this time, to write a *diamante* poem. Tell the class to be sure the words are carefully chosen to represent the concepts they are describing. Also, tell the students to be certain they choose the proper *length* for their words to form a diamond pattern upon completion.

Teacher's Note: This type of poem is an excellent choice because it enables students to write poetry without overly focusing on the traditional rules of poetry. Students like this activity, and they tend to consider their words very carefully, which is a trait they will continue when writing traditional poems.

Step 4 – Discussion: When the class has completed the diamante poems, select several students to read their poems aloud, and discuss them openly. Be certain to discuss the language used, especially words that produce clear images that readers can relate to, helping to make the meaning of the poems clear.

Step 5 – Assessment: As a homework assignment, have the students write two diamante poems on topics of their choosing, and tell them to be prepared to read the selected poems aloud in class. Students should be able to point out the reasons for the specific language they used, especially words producing imagery, and explain how the words help readers understand the meaning of each poem.

Onomatopoeia

Objective: To demonstrate to students how the poetic device of *onomatopoeia* helps the reader focus on images the poet creates, which better enables readers to understand the meanings of poems. Focusing on the selection of specific words to create imagery enables students to develop into writers that are more creative.

Step 1 – Warm-up: Ask students to write a short poem on any subject they choose. Tell them they must attempt to select several specific words in their poems that in and of themselves conjure up images in the minds of readers. For example, a word like *crash* will tend to move a reader's mind to specific instances in his or her life that are unique – and meaningful. When they have finished writing their poetry, select several students to read their poems aloud to the class, and have the class briefly comment and discuss them.

Step 2 – Introduction to the Lesson:
Following the warm-up, explain the nature of
the literary element of *onomatopoeia* to the
class:

onomatopoeia is the use of words that
imitate the sounds they describe.
The purpose of this poetic device is to focus
the attention of readers on images and moods
the poet intends to create. Identification of
these parts of a poem particularly important to
the poet helps readers to interpret the poet's
meaning.

Step 3 – Activity: *The Bells* by Edgar Allan
Poe is a famous onomatopoeic poem. Ask
students to read the following two stanzas from
the poem, paying particular attention to the
words the poet uses to create different scenes
for the reader using the technique of
onomatopoeia:

Hear the sledges with the bells
Silver bells!

What a world of merriment their melody
foretells!
How they tinkle, tinkle, tinkle,
In the icy air of night!
While the stars that oversprinkle
All the heavens, seem to twinkle
With a crystalline delight;
Keeping time, time, time,
In a sort of Runic rhyme,
To the tintinnabulation that so musically wells
From the bells, bells, bells, bells,
Bells, bells, bells
From the jingling and the tinkling of the bells.
Hear the mellow wedding bells,
Golden bells!
What a world of happiness their harmony
foretells!
Through the balmy air of night
How they ring out their delight!
From the molten-golden notes,
And all in tune,
What a liquid ditty floats
To the turtle-dove that listens, while she gloats
On the moon!

Oh, from out the sounding cells,

What a gush of euphony voluminously wells!

How it swells!

How it dwells

On the Future! how it tells

Of the rapture that impels

To the swinging and the ringing

Of the bells, bells, bells,

Of the bells, bells, bells, bells,

Bells, bells, bells

To the rhyming and the chiming of the bells!

Be certain students read the poem the first time for enjoyment only. On their second reading, have them make note of any use of onomatopoeia by the poet. After identifying onomatopoeia, ask them to write a short essay on how the meaning of the poem is made clearer by focusing on the images and moods discovered through the onomatopoeia found in the poem.

Teacher's Note: This poem is an excellent choice because it is replete with onomatopoeia.

Students will easily identify the repetition of sounds, forcing them to focus on Poe's imagery.

Step 4 – Discussion: When the class has completed the essays, select several students to read their essays aloud, and discuss them openly. Be certain to point out any onomatopoeia used, the resulting mood and imagery, and relate the use of sounds that suggest their meaning to the overall ease of understanding the poem.

Step 5 – Assessment: As a homework assignment, have the students write a poem using the literary device of onomatopoeia, and tell them to be prepared to read their selections aloud in class. Students should be able to point out the use of onomatopoeia in the stanzas they choose, and explain how it helps to explain the meaning of each stanza. Tell the class that each poem should contain at least five examples of onomatopoeia.

Haiku

Objective: To help students become more creative in their writing styles by allowing them to express feelings and moods in such a way as to paint pictures in poetic form for their readers, using very few, carefully-chosen words and phrases.

Step 1 – Warm-up: Ask students to write a short poem on the subject of nature. Tell them they must attempt to select very few specific words in their poems that paint images in the minds of their readers. For example, a word like *rainy* will tend to move a reader's mind to a narrow, identifiable concept. When they have finished writing their poetry, select several students to read their poems aloud to the class, and have the class briefly comment and discuss them.

Step 2 – Introduction to the Lesson: Following the warm-up, explain the nature of the literary genre of *haiku* to the class:

haiku is a Japanese poetic art form, containing one verse of no more than three lines, no rhymes, and only seventeen syllables. The three lines in the verse follow the 5-7-5 rule. This means that the first line contains five syllables, the second line seven syllables, and the third line five syllables. The genre is designed to convey deep thoughts and moods with very few words. Consequently, the words must be carefully selected.

Step 3 – Activity: The following haiku poem was written by a famous Japanese poet, who lived in the 17th century and is considered one of the fathers of this art form. Write this poem on the classroom whiteboard:

> This snowy morning
> That black crow I hate so much ....
> But he's beautiful!
>
> > by Basho

Ask the students to note the words that express moods, feelings, and deep thoughts.

Teacher's Note: This poem by Basho describes an image of winter. It is the snowy background that gives the black crow its beauty as described in the poem. The words *snowy, hate,* and *beautiful* are particularly effective.

After the class has commented on Basho's poem, ask the students to write their own haiku poems. The poems must adhere to the following rules:

    a. The subject matter must connect somehow to nature.

    b. The poems must express a mood, deep thought, or feeling in such a way as to make others see in their minds a picture or image being described.

    c. The poems must adhere to the 5-7-5 rule.

    d. The poems must not rhyme.

Step 4 – Discussion: When the class has completed the poems, select several students to read their poems aloud. Each time a poem is read, ask the class to draw a picture or sketch of the images expressed in the poem. Then, compare the images and drawings, and openly discuss them.

Step 5 – Assessment: As a homework assignment, have the students write at least three haiku poems, and tell them to be prepared to read their selections aloud in class. Students should be able to demonstrate an understanding of the genre, and the importance of careful word selection when writing creatively.

Poetry Project: A Dedication
(Two-Three 45-Minute Class Sessions)

Objective: Students will learn to read and interpret poems, to create accompanying illustrations for poems, and to create a poetry booklet that will serve as a dedication in verse form. The class will express sentiment through poetry.

Step 1 – Warm-up: Ask students to think about a person to whom they will dedicate this poetry project. Students should peruse magazines, the internet, poetry books, and other sources for ideas and poems to be used in connection with this project. A school media center is an ideal location for this exercise. Students should be specifically instructed to select poems that relate in some way to the person to whom the project is being dedicated. Each student should select at least 15 poems to be used in support of the dedication.

Step 2 – Introduction to the Lesson:

Following the warm-up, explain the nature of a poem used as a dedication to someone by having students read the following poem:

Washington's Birthday

by Margaret E. Sangster

'Tis splendid to have a record
So white and free from stain
That, held to the light, it shows no blot,
Though tested and tried amain;
That age to age forever
Repeats its story of love,
And your birthday lives in a nation's heart,
All other days above.

And this is Washington's glory,
A steadfast soul and true,
Who stood for his country's honor
When his country's days were few.
And now when its days are many,
And its flag of stars is flung

To the breeze in radiant glory,

His name is on every tongue.

Yes, it's splendid to live so bravely,

To be so great and strong,

That your memory is ever a tocsin

To rally the foes of wrong;

To live so proudly and purely,

That your people pause in their way,

And year by year, with banner and drum,

Keep the thought of your natal day.

Teacher's Note: Be certain students read the poem the first time for enjoyment only. On their second reading, have them make note of the language used by the poet in honoring Washington. This poem is an excellent choice because it is obvious the poet is dedicating her work as a tribute to the first president, with a myriad of historical references.

Step 3 – Activity: Following the warm-up, instruct the students to begin creating booklets of poems dedicated to a person of each student's choosing (as determined during the warm-up exercise). Collected poems, student poems, accompanying illustrations and drawings, explanations of choices, and personal responses will be accumulated into folders, which will serve as the dedication booklets. Students should be asked to:

1. Select the person to whom the project will be dedicated.

2. Select at least 15 poems in support of the dedication. Students should feel free to write their own poems as well.

3. Explain why each poem has been selected and how each poem supports the dedication.

4. Draw illustrations in support of the person to whom the booklet is dedicated, or affix illustrations from other sources (such as magazine cutouts).

5. Write a personal response to the overall dedication project.

Step 4 – Discussion: When the class has completed the projects, select students should read the contents of the booklets aloud to the class, and discuss them openly. Be certain to point out the relationship between the poems selected and the person to whom the booklet is dedicated.

Step 5 – Assessment: The dedication projects should be graded in four distinct categories: content, creativity, overall expression of sentimentality, and grammar & usage.

Poetry and Art

Objective: To demonstrate to students the relationship between poetry and art as expressive media forms. The similarities between poetry and art will help students interpret both forms of creative expression. This exercise is designed to approach poetry from the opposite perspective. Instead of reading a poem and conjuring up images in their minds, students are asked to view images and write poems on what they observe.

Step 1 – Warm-up: Ask students to select a work of art, preferably a painting. The art work can be shown as an LCD presentation in the classroom, an overhead transparency, a computer image, or a handout. Then, have them write a short poem on the images they see in the painting. When they have finished writing their poetry, select several students to read their poems aloud to the class, and have the class briefly comment and discuss them.

Step 2 – Introduction to the Lesson:
Following the warm-up, explain the following literary elements to the class:

poetry is writing that formulates a concentrated imaginative awareness of experience in language chosen and arranged to create a specific emotional response through meaning, sound, and rhythm. Explain to the class that while there is no single accepted definition for poetry, the above definition is commonly used in academic circles.

art is the conscious production or arrangement of sounds, colors, forms, movements, or other elements in a manner that affects the sense of beauty. Once again, explain to the class that while there is no single accepted definition for art, the above definition is commonly used in academic circles.

Discuss these definitions with the class, and solicit additional definitions from the students in order to get their input as to concepts they believe form all or part of these genres. Write the additional definitions or terms for each on the whiteboard for all to see.

Step 3 – Activity: Ask the students to repeat the process they used to write their poetry during the Warm-up session. Ask students to select a work of art, preferably a painting. The art work can be shown as an LCD presentation in the classroom, an overhead transparency, a computer image, or a handout. Then, have them write a short poem on the images they see in the painting or paintings selected. When they have finished writing their poetry, select several students to read their poems aloud to the class, and have the class briefly comment and discuss them.

Teacher's Note: There are no universally accepted definitions of *poetry* or *art*. However, both forms express emotion, and both may be interpreted in different ways by readers or viewers. Art tends to be more visual, while poetry uses language for expression. Both take advantage of meaning and sound. Poetry stresses rhythm, and art stresses movement. Both forms are creative, and allow recipients to expand their imaginations.

Step 4 – Discussion: When the class has completed the poems, select several students to read their poems aloud, and discuss them openly. Be certain to point out the relationship of the poems the students write to the visual depictions in the paintings, and discuss the overall meaning of both the poems written and art viewed.

Step 5 – Assessment: As a homework assignment, have the students select paintings of their choice, and write poems on the images they observe. Tell them to be prepared to read their poems aloud in class. They must bring in a copy of the paintings they have selected. Students should be able to explain the relationship between the painting and the poem.

I'm Terribly Sorry

Objective: To demonstrate to students through poetry how significant a simple apology can be to a meaningful relationship with friends and family members. This exercise is designed to show that poetry is a useful tool as a means of self-expression in situations where emotions play a role in relationships.

Step 1 – Warm-up: Ask students to write a paragraph or two about a situation in their lives when they either feel they should have given an apology to someone or received an apology from someone. Be sure to have them express what that apology would entail. When they have finished writing, select several students to read their paragraphs aloud to the class, and have the class briefly comment and discuss them.

Step 2 – Introduction to the Lesson:
Following the warm-up, explain the following definition to the class:

An **apology** is an expression of regret at having caused trouble for someone, having hurt someone, or having done something that adversely affected another person.

Explain to the class that while there is no single accepted definition for *apology*, the above definition is commonly used in the United States of America.

Discuss this definition with the class, and solicit additional definitions from the students in order to get their input as to concepts they believe form all or part of an expected apology. Write the additional definitions or terms for each on the whiteboard for all to see.

Step 3 – Activity: Ask the students to read the following poem by Ella Wheeler Wilcox:

There's one sad truth in life I've found
While journeying east and west-
The only folks we really wound

Are those we love the best.
We flatter those we scarcely know,
We please the fleeting guest,
And deal full many a thoughtless blow
To those who love us best.

Ask students to write a poem of apology to someone with whom they have or have had a meaningful relationship and offended in some way.

Be sure the students understand that their poems should satisfy the definitions of *apology* discussed during the introduction to the lesson.

Teacher's Note: The above untitled poem by Ella Wheeler Wilcox is particularly effective for this lesson because students will identify with the universal truth that we tend to hurt the ones we love. Especially when we are young, we tend to treat strangers more kindly and with more respect than we do our friends and family members.

Step 4 – Discussion: When the class has completed the poems, select several students to read their poems aloud, and discuss them openly. Be certain to point out the relationship between the poems the class has written and the definitions of apology the class has adopted.

Step 5 – Assessment: As a homework assignment, have the students write poems on the apologies they would like to receive from others. Tell them to be prepared to read their poems aloud in class. Students should be able to explain the relationship between the incident that offended them and the poems of apology they have written.

Poetry from Prose

Objective: This exercise is designed to allow students working in small groups to focus on the words and phrases used in descriptive prose passages. Students will have an opportunity to understand the effects of word usage in the prose they read and to think more creatively when writing their own prose selections. In addition, students will learn to distinguish prose from poetry.

Step 1 – Warm-up: In this exercise, students are given prose excerpts from famous works of literature. The prose may be short selections written on a whiteboard, handouts distributed to the class, or selections from textbooks, novels, or short stories available in the classroom. Begin by telling the class to read the prose selection once in its entirety. When the class has finished, direct the students to re-read the selection, highlighting, underlining, or listing on a separate sheet of paper at least twenty-five words or phrases they believe to be the most significant, descriptive, and essential to the prose selection.

When the lists of words and phrases are complete, select several students to read their lists aloud to the class, and have the class briefly comment and discuss them. Open the discussion to the class to exchange the collective thoughts of the students on the process of selecting the particular words and phrases chosen, and the effectiveness of the chosen words and phrases.

Step 2 – Introduction to the Lesson:
Following the warm-up, explain the following literary elements to the class:

poetry is writing that formulates a concentrated imaginative awareness of experience in language chosen and arranged to create a specific emotional response through meaning, sound, and rhythm. Explain to the class that while there is no single accepted definition for poetry, the above definition is commonly used in academic circles.

prose is ordinary writing, distinguished from verse, that resembles everyday speech. Unlike poetry, it is non-metered, unrhymed language consisting of logically related sentences. Once again, explain to the class that while there is no single accepted definition for prose, the above definition is commonly used in academic circles.

Discuss these definitions with the class, and solicit additional definitions from the students in order to get their input as to concepts they believe form all or part of these genres. Write the additional definitions or terms for each on the whiteboard for all to see. Students should be directed to use these definitions as guides when participating in the following class activity.

Step 3 – Activity: Following the introduction to the lesson, when each student's word/phrase list is complete, instruct the class to write a poem, using any style, containing the words and phrases they have extracted from the prose selection during the warm-up session in Step 1 above. The poem may be any length, but every word or phrase taken from the prose selection must be used. Students may change tenses and punctuation and add their own words to make the poem flow, but no more than three of their own words per line may be used.

Teacher's Note: Remember, this activity is best performed in small groups. As a guide for this activity, consider using the following excerpt from Chapter Two of Mark Twain's novel, *Tom Sawyer*:

"SATURDAY morning was come, and all **the summer world was bright and fresh,** and brimming with life. There was **a song in every heart;** and if the heart was young the music issued at the lips. There was cheer in every face and a spring in every step. The locust-trees were in bloom and the fragrance of the blossoms filled the air. Cardiff Hill, beyond the village and above it, was green with vegetation and it lay just far enough away to seem a Delectable Land, **dreamy, reposeful, and inviting.**

Tom appeared on the sidewalk with a bucket of whitewash and a long-handled brush. He surveyed the fence, and all **gladness** left him and a **deep melancholy** settled down upon his spirit. **Thirty yards of board fence nine feet high.** Life to him **seemed** hollow, and existence **but a burden.** Sighing, he dipped his brush and passed it along the topmost plank; repeated the operation; did it again; compared the insignificant whitewashed streak with the far-reaching continent of unwhitewashed fence, and sat down on a tree-box discouraged. Jim came skipping out at the gate with a tin pail, and singing Buffalo Gals. Bringing water from the town pump had always been hateful work in Tom's eyes, before, but now it did not strike him so. He remembered that there was company at the pump. White, mulatto, and negro boys and girls were always there waiting their turns, resting, trading playthings, quarrelling, fighting, skylarking. And he remembered that although the pump was only a hundred and fifty yards off, Jim never got back with a bucket of water under an hour -- and even then somebody generally had to go after him."

A typical first stanza of a student poem might look like this:

The summer world is bright and fresh
With songs in every heart, dreamy, reposeful,
*   and inviting.*
But gladness becomes melancholy
When thirty yards of board fence nine feet
*   high*
Seems but a burden, not exciting.

Step 4 – Discussion: After the class has completed its poetry, ask for student volunteers to read their poetry aloud to the class. Allow for plenty of discussion on the resultant poems, their possible meanings, and the thought patterns generated. Be certain to discuss whether the poems created change the meaning intended in the original prose passage.

Step 5 – Assessment: As a homework assignment, have the students select another literature excerpt of their choice and perform the activity of extracting words and phrases and creating poems in the same manner as they did in class. Tell them to be certain to produce a word/phrase list *prior* to the writing of their poems. They should be prepared to discuss both their word/phrase lists and their poetry drafts in the next class. Teachers will be able to recognize how the class has improved its understanding of the significance of choosing the proper words and phrases when writing prose. Teachers will see that students performing this exercise learn how prose writers, like poets, must carefully choose their words and phrases to generate effective descriptions.

Prose

Prose from Poetry

Objective: This exercise is designed to allow students working in small groups to focus on the words and phrases used in descriptive poetry and prose passages. Students will have an opportunity to understand the effects of word usage in the poetry they read, to recognize that prose writers follow similar rules for word usage when attempting to produce a desired effect, and to think more creatively when writing their own prose selections. In addition, students will learn to identify the similarities between poetry and prose.

Step 1 – Warm-up: In this exercise, students are given famous works of poetry to explore. The poetry may be a short selection written on a whiteboard, handouts distributed to the class, or a selection from textbooks available in the classroom. Begin by telling the class to read the poem selected once in its entirety. When the class has finished, direct the students to re-read the selection, highlighting, underlining, or listing on a separate sheet of paper at least fifteen words or phrases they believe to be the most significant, descriptive, and essential to the poetry selection.

When the lists of words and phrases are complete, select several students to read their lists aloud to the class, and have the class briefly comment and discuss them. Open the discussion to the class to exchange the collective thoughts of the students on the process of selecting the particular words and phrases chosen, and the effectiveness of the chosen words and phrases.

Step 2 – Introduction to the Lesson:
Following the warm-up, explain the following literary elements to the class:

poetry is writing that formulates a concentrated imaginative awareness of experience in language chosen and arranged to create a specific emotional response through meaning, sound, and rhythm. Explain to the class that while there is no single accepted definition for poetry, the above definition is commonly used in academic circles.

prose is ordinary writing, distinguished from verse, that resembles everyday speech. Unlike poetry, it is non-metered, unrhymed language consisting of logically related sentences. Once again, explain to the class that while there is no single accepted definition for prose, the above definition is commonly used in academic circles.

Discuss these definitions with the class, and solicit additional definitions from the students in order to get their input as to concepts they believe form all or part of these genres. Write the additional definitions or terms for each on the whiteboard for all to see. Students should be directed to use these definitions as guides when participating in the following class activity.

Step 3 – Activity: Following the introduction to the lesson, when each student's word/phrase list is complete, instruct the class to write a short essay containing the words and phrases they have extracted from the poetry selection during the warm-up session in Step 1 above. The essay may be any length, but every word or phrase taken from the poetry selection must be used. Students may change tenses and punctuation and add their own words to make the essay flow.

Teacher's Note: Remember, this activity is best performed in small groups. As a guide for this activity, consider using the following poem, *The Road Not Taken*:

Two roads diverged in a yellow wood,
And sorry I could not travel both
And be one traveler, long I stood
And looked down one as far as I could
To where it bent in the undergrowth.
Then took the other, as just as fair,
And having perhaps the better claim,

Because it was grassy and wanted wear;
Though as for that the passing there
Had worn them really about the same.

And both that morning equally lay
In leaves no step had trodden black.
Oh, I kept the first for another day!
Yet knowing how way leads on to way,
I doubted if I should ever come back.

I shall be telling this with a sigh
Somewhere ages and ages hence:
Two roads diverged in a wood, and I--
I took the one less traveled by,
And that has made all the difference.

by *Robert Frost*

Step 4 – Discussion: After the class has
completed its essays, ask for student volunteers
to read their essays aloud to the class. Allow for
plenty of discussion on the resultant prose,
their possible meanings, and the thought
patterns generated. Be certain to discuss

whether the prose created changed the meaning intended in the original poetry passage.

Step 5 – Assessment: As a homework assignment, have the students select another poem of their choice and perform the activity of extracting words and phrases and creating prose in the same manner as they did in class. Tell them to be certain to produce a word/phrase list *prior* to the writing of their essays. They should be prepared to discuss both their word/phrase lists and their prose drafts in the next class. Teachers will be able to recognize how the class has improved its understanding of the significance of choosing the proper words and phrases when writing prose. Teachers will see that students performing this exercise learn how prose writers, like poets, must carefully choose their words and phrases to generate effective descriptions.

The Great Gatsby

Objective: This exercise is designed to allow students to examine the major theme of achieving the American dream as presented in F. Scott Fitzgerald's classic novel, *The Great Gatsby*. Students will have an opportunity to understand the connection between major themes found in classic prose literature and contemporary American society, and to incorporate similar themes when writing their own prose selections.

Step 1 – Warm-up: In this exercise, students are asked to write a short essay on their understanding of the American dream. They should consider whether it encompasses material things, spiritual enlightenment, physical health, money, power, etc.

When the short essays are complete, select several students to read their essays aloud to the class, and have the class briefly comment and discuss them. Open the discussion to the class to exchange the collective thoughts of the students on the process of selecting the elements they believe comprise the satisfactory achievement of their version of the American dream.

Step 2 – Introduction to the Lesson:
Following the warm-up, explain the following concept to the class:

   American Dream: In the 21st century, it is generally believed that the widespread aspiration of Americans to live better, more fulfilling lives than their parents did with an improved quality of life is the ultimate American dream.

   Discuss the above definition with the class, and solicit additional definitions from the students based on their warm-up activity in order to get their input. Write the additional definitions or terms on the whiteboard for all to see. Students should be directed to use these definitions as guides when participating in the following class activity.

Step 3 – Activity: Following the introduction to the lesson, when each student has formed an opinion about the American dream, instruct the class to write a short essay on their personal long-term goals for their own lives, considering the warm-up session in Step 1 above, and the conclusions arrived at in Step 2 above. The essay may be any length. Explain to the class that in the novel, *The Great Gatsby,* the narrator, Nick Carraway, demonstrates the disgust he feels for the people surrounding Gatsby's life. He believes the life of the wealthy produces moral decay and emptiness, contrary to the American dream. Confront the class with this conflict: If wealth produces hollowness in life, what should they strive for when attempting to meet their personal goals?

Teacher's Note: This activity may be molded to any classic work of literature by simply selecting a major theme in a novel and having the class relate the theme to their personal lives.

Step 4 – Discussion: After the class has completed its essays, ask for student volunteers to read their essays aloud to the class. Allow for plenty of discussion on the resultant goals. Be sure to discuss the thought patterns generated. Attempt to reach accord in the class, (which is very difficult), and make certain the students provide alternative solutions to the dilemma posed by the exercise.

Step 5 – Assessment: As a homework assignment, have the students select a descriptive passage or scene from *The Great Gatsby*. Ask them to create an artistic piece demonstrating the passage or scene they have selected. The artwork may be a drawing, painting, musical composition, or any creative expression of choice.

They should be prepared to discuss their selection, the reason for the selection, and the resultant artwork in the next class. Teachers will be able to recognize how the class has understood the major theme of "the American dream" in the chosen text by viewing the artistic expressions of the students, and paying attention to the reasoning set forth in the student discussions surrounding their art production.

Short Story Elements: Setting
(One-Two 45-Minute Class Sessions)

Objective: This exercise is designed to allow students to examine one of the major elements of a short story. Students will have an opportunity to understand the connection between the setting found in classic prose literature and contemporary American society, and to focus on setting when writing their own prose selections.

Step 1 – Warm-up: In this exercise, students are asked to write a short story on a topic of their choice. They should consider ordinary, everyday happenings in their lives as the subject matter of their stories. Due to the time constraints, the short stories written for the purposes of this warm-up will be of essay length.

When the short stories are complete, select several students to read their prose aloud to the class, and have the class briefly comment and

discuss them. Open the discussion to the class to exchange the collective thoughts of the students on the process of selecting the elements they believe comprise the satisfactory achievement of their version of a short story.

Step 2 – Introduction to the Lesson:
Following the warm-up, explain the following concepts to the class:

short story: A short story is the telling of a happening or a series of events. It is also a narrative designed to interest, amuse, or inform the reader.

setting: The time and location in which a story takes place is called the setting. For some stories the setting is very important, while for others it is not. There are several aspects of a story's setting to consider when examining how setting contributes to a story. Some, or all, may be present in a story.

Setting Considerations:

a) place - geographical location. Where is the action of the story taking place?

b) time - When is the story taking place? (historical period, time of day, year, etc.)

c) weather conditions - Is it rainy, sunny, stormy, etc?

d) social conditions - What is the daily life of the characters like? Does the story contain local color (writing that focuses on the speech, dress, mannerisms, customs, etc. of a particular place)?

e) mood or atmosphere - What feeling is created at the beginning of the story? Is it bright and cheerful or dark and frightening?

Discuss the above definition with the class, and solicit additional definitions from the students based on their warm-up activity in order to get their input. Write the additional definitions or terms on the whiteboard for all to see. Students should be directed to use these definitions as guides when participating in the following class activity.

Step 3 – Activity: Following the introduction to the lesson, when each student has formed an opinion about the elements of a short story, instruct the class to write a fictionalized short story based on their personal lives. While considering the warm-up session in Step 1 above and the conclusions arrived at in Step 2 above, the class should be instructed to focus its attention on the short story element of *setting* for this assignment. The short story may be any length, and at the teacher's discretion, may encompass more than one class session.

Teacher's Note: This activity may be molded to any modern short story or classic work of literature by simply selecting the story, examining the setting, and directing the class to write a similar tale based on their own experiences.

Step 4 – Discussion: After the class has completed its short stories, ask for student volunteers to read their prose aloud to the class. Allow for plenty of discussion on the treatment of setting. Be sure to discuss the thought patterns generated. Make certain the students in the class provide alternative settings for each story, and discuss how changing the setting might change the story itself.

Step 5 – Assessment: As a homework assignment, have the students select a descriptive passage or scene from a short story of their choice. Ask them to create an artistic piece demonstrating the passage or scene they have selected. The artwork may be a drawing, painting, musical composition, or any creative expression of choice. They should be prepared to discuss their selection, the reason for the selection, and the resultant artwork in the next class. Teachers will be able to recognize how the class has understood the concept of *setting* by viewing the artistic expressions of the students, and paying attention to the reasoning set forth in the student discussions surrounding their art production.

Short Story Elements: Plot
(One-Two 45-Minute Class Sessions)

Objective: This exercise is designed to allow students to examine one of the major elements of a short story. Students will have an opportunity to understand the connection between the plot found in classic prose literature and contemporary American society, and to focus on plot when writing their own prose selections.

Step 1 – Warm-up: In this exercise, students are asked to write a short story on a topic of their choice. They should consider ordinary, everyday happenings in their lives as the subject matter of their stories. Due to the time constraints, the short stories written for the purposes of this warm-up will be of essay length.

When the short stories are complete, select several students to read their prose aloud to the class, and have the class briefly comment and

discuss them. Open the discussion to the class to exchange the collective thoughts of the students on the process of selecting the elements they believe comprise the satisfactory achievement of their version of a short story.

Step 2 – Introduction to the Lesson:
Following the warm-up, explain the following concepts to the class:

short story: A short story is the telling of a happening or a series of events. It is also a narrative designed to interest, amuse, or inform the reader.

plot: The plot is how the author arranges events to develop his basic idea; It is the sequence of events in a story or play. The plot is a planned, logical series of events having a beginning, middle, and end. The short story usually has one plot so it can be read in one sitting. There are five essential parts of plot.

Essential Elements of Plot:

a) Introduction - The beginning of the story where the characters and the setting are revealed.

b) Rising Action - This is where the events in the story become complicated and the conflict in the story is revealed (events between the introduction and climax).

c) Climax - This is the highest point of interest and the turning point of the story. The reader wonders what will happen next; will the conflict be resolved or not?

d) Falling action - The events and complications begin to resolve themselves. The reader knows what has happened next and if the conflict was resolved or not (events between climax and denouement).

e) Denouement - This is the final outcome or untangling of events in the story.

Discuss the above definitions and concepts with the class, and solicit additional definitions from the students based on their warm-up activity in order to get their input. Write the additional definitions or terms on the whiteboard for all to see. Students should be directed to use these definitions as guides when participating in the following class activity.

Step 3 – Activity: Following the introduction to the lesson, when each student has formed an opinion about the elements of a short story, instruct the class to write a fictionalized short story based on their personal lives. While considering the warm-up session in Step 1 above and the conclusions arrived at in Step 2 above, the class should be instructed to focus its attention on the short story element of *plot* for this assignment. The short story may be any length, and at the teacher's discretion, may encompass more than one class session.

Teacher's Note: This activity may be molded to any modern short story or classic work of literature by simply selecting the story, examining the plot, and directing the class to write a similar tale based on their own experiences.

Step 4 – Discussion: After the class has completed its short stories, ask for student volunteers to read their prose aloud to the class. Allow for plenty of discussion on the treatment of plot. Be sure to discuss the thought patterns generated. Make certain the students in the class provide alternative plots for each story, and discuss how changing the plot might change the impact of the short story on the reader.

Step 5 – Assessment: As a homework assignment, have the students select a significant passage or scene from a short story of their choice. Ask them to create an artistic piece demonstrating the passage or scene they have selected. The artwork may be a drawing, painting, musical composition, or any creative expression of choice.

They should be prepared to discuss their selection, the reason for the selection, and the resultant artwork in the next class. Teachers will be able to recognize how the class has understood the concept of *plot* by viewing the artistic expressions of the students, and paying attention to the reasoning set forth in the student discussions surrounding their art production.

Short Story Elements: Conflict
(One-Two 45-Minute Class Sessions)

Objective: This exercise is designed to allow students to examine one of the major elements of a short story. Students will have an opportunity to understand the connection between the conflict found in classic prose literature and contemporary American society, and to focus on conflict when writing their own prose selections.

Step 1 – Warm-up: In this exercise, students are asked to write a short story on a topic of their choice. They should consider ordinary, everyday happenings in their lives as the subject matter of their stories. Due to the time constraints, the short stories written for the purposes of this warm-up will be of essay length.

When the short stories are complete, select several students to read their prose aloud to the class, and have the class briefly comment and

discuss them. Open the discussion to the class to exchange the collective thoughts of the students on the process of selecting the elements they believe comprise the satisfactory achievement of their version of a short story.

Step 2 – Introduction to the Lesson:
Following the warm-up, explain the following concepts to the class:

short story: A short story is the telling of a happening or a series of events. It is also a narrative designed to interest, amuse, or inform the reader.

conflict: Conflict is essential to plot. Without conflict there is no plot. It is the opposition of forces, which ties one incident to another and makes the plot move. Conflict is not merely limited to open arguments; rather it is any form of opposition that faces the main character. Within a short story, there may be only one central struggle, or there may be one dominant struggle with many minor ones.

Types of Conflict:

1) External - A struggle with a force outside one's self.

2) Internal - A struggle within one's self; a person must make some decision, overcome pain, quiet his or her temper, resist an urge, etc.

Discuss the above definitions and concepts with the class, and solicit additional definitions from the students based on their warm-up activity in order to get their input. Write the additional definitions or terms on the whiteboard for all to see. Students should be directed to use these definitions as guides when participating in the following class activity.

Step 3 – Activity: Following the introduction to the lesson, when each student has formed an opinion about the elements of a short story, instruct the class to write a fictionalized short story based on their personal lives. While considering the warm-up session in Step 1 above and the conclusions arrived at in Step 2 above, the class should be instructed to focus its attention on the short story element of *conflict* for this assignment. The short story may be any length, and at the teacher's discretion, may encompass more than one class session.

Teacher's Note: This activity may be molded to any modern short story or classic work of literature by simply selecting the story, examining the conflict in the plot, and directing the class to write a similar tale based on their own experiences.

Step 4 – Discussion: After the class has completed its short stories, ask for student volunteers to read their prose aloud to the class. Allow for plenty of discussion on the treatment of conflict. Be sure to discuss the thought patterns generated. Make certain the students in the class provide alternative conflicts for each story, and discuss how changing the conflict might change the outcome of the short story and its impact on the reader.

Step 5 – Assessment: As a homework assignment, have the students select a significant passage or scene from a short story of their choice. Ask them to create an artistic piece demonstrating the passage or scene they have selected. The artwork may be a drawing, painting, musical composition, or any creative expression of choice.

They should be prepared to discuss their selection, the reason for the selection, and the resultant artwork in the next class. Teachers will be able to recognize how the class has understood the concept of *conflict* by viewing the artistic expressions of the students, and paying attention to the reasoning set forth in the student discussions surrounding their art production.

Short Story Elements: Character
(One-Two 45-Minute Class Sessions)

Objective: This exercise is designed to allow students to examine one of the major elements of a short story. Students will have an opportunity to understand the connection between the characters found in classic prose literature and contemporary American society, and to focus on character development when writing their own prose selections.

Step 1 – Warm-up: In this exercise, students are asked to write a short story on a topic of their choice. They should consider ordinary, everyday happenings in their lives as the subject matter of their stories. Due to the time constraints, the short stories written for the purposes of this warm-up will be of essay length.

When the short stories are complete, select several students to read their prose aloud to the class, and have the class briefly comment and

discuss them. Open the discussion to the class to exchange the collective thoughts of the students on the process of selecting the elements they believe comprise the satisfactory achievement of their version of a short story.

Step 2 – Introduction to the Lesson:
Following the warm-up, explain the following concepts to the class:

short story: A short story is the telling of a happening or a series of events. It is also a narrative designed to interest, amuse, or inform the reader.

character: There are two meanings for the word character:

1) The person in a work of fiction.

2) The characteristics of a person.

characters in short stories (usually, very few):

Protagonist: The character clearly central to the story with all major events having some importance to this character (The Hero!)

Antagonist: The one opposing the main character

characteristics of a person: In order for a story to seem real to the reader its characters must seem real. Characterization is the information the author gives the reader about the characters themselves. The author may reveal a character in several ways:

a) his/her physical appearance

b) what he/she says, thinks, feels and dreams

c) what he/she does or does not do

d) what others say about him/her and how others react to him/her

Discuss the above definitions and concepts with the class, and solicit additional definitions from the students based on their warm-up activity in order to get their input. Write the additional definitions or terms on the whiteboard for all to see. Students should be directed to use these definitions as guides when participating in the following class activity.

Step 3 – Activity: Following the introduction to the lesson, when each student has formed an opinion about the elements of a short story, instruct the class to write a fictionalized short story based on their personal lives. While considering the warm-up session in Step 1 above and the conclusions arrived at in Step 2 above, the class should be instructed to focus its attention on the short story element of *character* and *character development* for this assignment. The short story may be any length, and at the teacher's discretion, may encompass more than one class session.

Teacher's Note: This activity may be molded to any modern short story or classic work of literature by simply selecting the story, examining the characters in the story, and directing the class to write a similar tale based on their own experiences.

Step 4 – Discussion: After the class has completed its short stories, ask for student volunteers to read their prose aloud to the class. Allow for plenty of discussion on the treatment of character. Be sure to discuss the thought patterns generated. Make certain the students in the class provide alternative characters for each story, and discuss how changing the characters might change the outcome of the short story and its impact on the reader.

Step 5 – Assessment: As a homework assignment, have the students select a significant passage or scene from a short story of their choice, which passage contains significant references to a particular character or characters. Ask them to create an artistic piece demonstrating the passage or scene they have selected. The artwork may be a drawing, painting, musical composition, or any creative expression of choice.

They should be prepared to discuss their selection, the reason for the selection, and the resultant artwork in the next class. Teachers will be able to recognize how the class has understood the concept of *character* by viewing the artistic expressions of the students, and paying attention to the reasoning set forth in the student discussions surrounding their art production.

Short Story Elements: Point of View
(One-Two 45-Minute Class Sessions)

Objective: This exercise is designed to allow students to examine one of the major elements of a short story. Students will have an opportunity to understand the connection between the author's *point of view* found in classic prose literature and contemporary American society, and to focus on *point of view* when writing their own prose selections.

Step 1 – Warm-up: In this exercise, students are asked to write a short story on a topic of their choice. They should consider ordinary, everyday happenings in their lives as the subject matter of their stories. Due to the time constraints, the short stories written for the purposes of this warm-up will be of essay length.

When the short stories are complete, select several students to read their prose aloud to the class, and have the class briefly comment and

discuss them. Open the discussion to the class to exchange the collective thoughts of the students on the process of selecting the elements they believe comprise the satisfactory achievement of their version of a short story.

Step 2 – Introduction to the Lesson:
Following the warm-up, explain the following concepts to the class:

short story: A short story is the telling of a happening or a series of events. It is also a narrative designed to interest, amuse, or inform the reader.

point of view (POV): Point of View is defined as the angle from which the story is told.

first person: The story is told by the protagonist or one of the characters who interacts closely with the protagonist or other characters (using pronouns I, me, we, etc). The reader sees the story through this person's eyes as he/she experiences it and only knows what he/she knows or feels.

Omniscient: The author can narrate the story using the omniscient point of view. He can move from character to character, event to event, having free access to the thoughts, feelings and motivations of his characters and he introduces information where and when he chooses.

Discuss the above definitions and concepts with the class, and solicit additional definitions from the students based on their warm-up activity in order to get their input. Write the additional definitions or terms on the whiteboard for all to see. Students should be directed to use these definitions as guides when participating in the following class activity.

Step 3 – Activity: Following the introduction to the lesson, when each student has formed an opinion about the elements of a short story, instruct the class to write a fictionalized short story based on their personal lives. While considering the warm-up session in Step 1 above and the conclusions arrived at in Step 2 above, the class should be instructed to focus its attention on the short story element of *point of view* for this assignment. The short story may be any length, and at the teacher's discretion, may encompass more than one class session.

Teacher's Note: This activity may be molded to any modern short story or classic work of literature by simply selecting the story, examining the *point of view* in the story, and directing the class to write a similar tale based on their own experiences.

Step 4 – Discussion: After the class has completed its short stories, ask for student volunteers to read their prose aloud to the class. Allow for plenty of discussion on the author's *point of view*. Be sure to discuss the thought patterns generated. Make certain the students in the class provide alternative *points* *of view* for each story, and discuss how changing the *point of view* might change the outcome of the short story and its impact on the reader.

Step 5 – Assessment: As a homework assignment, have the students select a significant passage or scene from a short story of their choice, which passage demonstrates a particular *point of view*. Ask them to create an artistic piece demonstrating the passage or scene they have selected. The artwork may be a drawing, painting, musical composition, or any creative expression of choice.

They should be prepared to discuss their selection, the reason for the selection, and the resultant artwork in the next class. Teachers will be able to recognize how the class has understood the concept of *point of view* by viewing the artistic expressions of the students, and paying attention to the reasoning set forth in the student discussions surrounding their art production.

Short Story Elements: Theme
(One-Two 45-Minute Class Sessions)

Objective: This exercise is designed to allow students to examine one of the major elements of a short story. Students will have an opportunity to understand the connection between the *themes* found in classic prose literature and contemporary American society, and to focus on *theme* when writing their own prose selections.

Step 1 – Warm-up: In this exercise, students are asked to write a short story on a topic of their choice. They should consider ordinary, everyday happenings in their lives as the subject matter of their stories. Due to the time constraints, the short stories written for the purposes of this warm-up will be of essay length.

When the short stories are complete, select several students to read their prose aloud to the class, and have the class briefly comment and

discuss them. Open the discussion to the class to exchange the collective thoughts of the students on the process of selecting the elements they believe comprise the satisfactory achievement of their version of a short story.

Step 2 – Introduction to the Lesson:
Following the warm-up, explain the following concepts to the class:

short story: A short story is the telling of a happening or a series of events. It is also a narrative designed to interest, amuse, or inform the reader.

theme: The theme in a piece of fiction is its controlling idea or its central insight. It is the author's underlying meaning or main idea that he is trying to convey. The theme may be the author's thoughts about a topic or view of human nature. The title of the short story usually points to what the writer is saying and he or she may use various figures of speech to emphasize the theme, such as, symbol, allusion, simile, metaphor, hyperbole, or irony.

Discuss the above definitions and concepts with the class, and solicit additional definitions from the students based on their warm-up activity in order to get their input. Write the additional definitions or terms on the whiteboard for all to see. Students should be directed to use these definitions as guides when participating in the following class activity.

Step 3 – Activity: Following the introduction to the lesson, when each student has formed an opinion about the elements of a short story, instruct the class to write a fictionalized short story based on their personal lives. While considering the warm-up session in Step 1 above and the conclusions arrived at in Step 2 above, the class should be instructed to focus its attention on the short story element of *theme* for this assignment. The short story may be any length, and at the teacher's discretion, may encompass more than one class session.

Teacher's Note: This activity may be molded to any modern short story or classic work of literature by simply selecting the story, examining the *theme* in the story, and directing the class to write a similar tale based on their own experiences.

Step 4 – Discussion: After the class has completed its short stories, ask for student volunteers to read their prose aloud to the class. Allow for plenty of discussion on the author's *theme*. Be sure to discuss the thought patterns generated. Make certain the students in the class provide alternative *themes* for each story, and discuss how changing the *theme* might change the impact on the reader.

Step 5 – Assessment: As a homework assignment, have the students select a significant passage or scene from a short story of their choice, which passage demonstrates a particular *theme*. Ask them to create an artistic piece demonstrating the passage or scene they have selected. The artwork may be a drawing, painting, musical composition, or any creative expression of choice.

They should be prepared to discuss their selection, the reason for the selection, and the resultant artwork in the next class. Teachers will be able to recognize how the class has understood the concept of *theme* by viewing the artistic expressions of the students, and paying attention to the reasoning set forth in the student discussions surrounding their art production.

Short Story Elements: Voice
(One-Two 45-Minute Class Sessions)

Objective: This exercise is designed to allow students to examine one of the major elements of a short story. Students will have an opportunity to understand the connection between the author's *voice* found in classic prose literature and contemporary American society, and to focus on *voice* when writing their own prose selections.

Step 1 – Warm-up: In this exercise, students are asked to write a short story on a topic of their choice. They should consider ordinary, everyday happenings in their lives as the subject matter of their stories. Due to the time constraints, the short stories written for the purposes of this warm-up will be of essay length.

When the short stories are complete, select several students to read their prose aloud to the class, and have the class briefly comment and

discuss them. Open the discussion to the class to exchange the collective thoughts of the students on the process of selecting the elements they believe comprise the satisfactory achievement of their version of a short story.

Step 2 – Introduction to the Lesson:
Following the warm-up, explain the following concepts to the class:

short story: A short story is the telling of a happening or a series of events. It is also a narrative designed to interest, amuse, or inform the reader.

voice: Voice refers to *how* an author tells a story. Voice is the manner in which you combine your ideas and language to create an effect. It is rhythm, tone, and style.

Discuss the above definitions and concepts with the class, and solicit additional definitions from the students based on their warm-up activity in order to get their input.

Write the additional definitions or terms on the whiteboard for all to see. Students should be directed to use these definitions as guides when participating in the following class activity.

Step 3 – Activity: Following the introduction to the lesson, when each student has formed an opinion about the elements of a short story, instruct the class to write a fictionalized short story based on their personal lives. While considering the warm-up session in Step 1 above and the conclusions arrived at in Step 2 above, the class should be instructed to focus its attention on the short story element of *voice* for this assignment. The short story may be any length, and at the teacher's discretion, may encompass more than one class session.

Teacher's Note: This activity may be molded to any modern short story or classic work of literature by simply selecting the story, examining the *voice* in the story, and directing the class to write a similar tale based on their own experiences.

Step 4 – Discussion: After the class has completed its short stories, ask for student volunteers to read their prose aloud to the class. Allow for plenty of discussion on the author's *voice*. Be sure to discuss the thought patterns generated. Make certain the students in the class provide alternative *voices* for each story, and discuss how changing the *voice* might change the impact on the reader.

Step 5 – Assessment: As a homework assignment, have the students select a significant passage or scene from a short story of their choice, which passage demonstrates a particular *voice* used by the author. Ask them to create an artistic piece demonstrating the passage or scene they have selected. The artwork may be a drawing, painting, musical composition, or any creative expression of choice.

They should be prepared to discuss their selection, the reason for the selection, and the resultant artwork in the next class. Teachers will be able to recognize how the class has understood the concept of *voice* by viewing the artistic expressions of the students, and paying attention to the reasoning set forth in the student discussions surrounding their art production.

Elements of Fiction: Irony
(One-Two 45-Minute Class Sessions)

Objective: This exercise is designed to allow students to examine one of the major elements of fiction prose. Students will have an opportunity to understand the connection between *irony* found in prose literature and contemporary American society, and to focus on *irony* when writing their own prose selections.

Step 1 – Warm-up: In this exercise, students are asked to write a short story on a topic of their choice. They should consider ordinary, everyday happenings *that did not go the way they planned* in their lives as the subject matter of their stories. Due to the time constraints, the short stories written for the purposes of this warm-up will be of essay length.

When the short stories are complete, select several students to read their prose aloud to the class, and have the class briefly comment and

discuss them. Open the discussion to the class to exchange the collective thoughts of the students on the process of selecting the elements they believe comprise the satisfactory achievement of their version of a short story.

Step 2 – Introduction to the Lesson:
Following the warm-up, explain the following concepts to the class:

irony: The contrast between what seems to be and what really is.

Discuss the above definition with the class, and solicit additional definitions from the students based on their warm-up activity in order to get their input. Write the additional definitions or terms on the whiteboard for all to see. (Using the simple definition above, teachers should be able to refer to multiple examples of irony found in classic and contemporary literature in order to direct and extend the class discussion). Students should be directed to use these definitions as guides when participating in the following class activity.

Step 3 – Activity: Following the introduction to the lesson, when each student has formed an opinion about the element of irony in fiction prose literature, instruct the class to write a fictionalized short story based on their personal lives. While considering the warm-up session in Step 1 above and the conclusions arrived at in Step 2 above, the class should be instructed to focus its attention on the element of *irony* used in fiction prose for this assignment. The short story may be any length, and at the teacher's discretion, may encompass more than one class session.

Teacher's Note: It is very helpful for the teacher to discuss irony found in popular movies and television shows. The discussion will make it easier to clarify the concept to the class – and students tend to love this exercise!

Step 4 – Discussion: After the class has completed its short stories, ask for student volunteers to read their prose aloud to the class. Allow for plenty of discussion on the use of *irony*. Be sure to discuss the thought patterns generated. Make certain the students in the class provide alternative possibilities for the use of *irony* in each story read, and discuss how changing the example of *irony* might change the impact on the reader.

Step 5 – Assessment: As a homework assignment, have the students select a significant passage or scene from a short story of their choice, which passage demonstrates the use of *irony*. Ask them to create an artistic piece demonstrating the passage or scene they have selected. The artwork may be a drawing, painting, musical composition, or any creative expression of choice, such as a mask, a collage of facial expressions, or newspaper clippings.

They should be prepared to discuss their selection, the reason for the selection, and the resultant artwork in the next class. Teachers will be able to recognize how the class has understood the concept of *irony* by viewing the artistic expressions of the students, and paying attention to the reasoning set forth in the student discussions surrounding their art production.

Elements of Fiction: Symbolism
(One-Two 45-Minute Class Sessions)

Objective: This exercise is designed to allow students to examine one of the major elements of fiction prose. Students will have an opportunity to understand the connection between *symbolism* found in prose literature and contemporary American society, and to focus on *symbolism* when writing their own prose selections.

Step 1 – Warm-up: In this exercise, students are asked to write a short story on a topic of their choice. They should consider ordinary, everyday persons, places, things, or events in their lives as the subject matter of their stories. Due to the time constraints, the short stories written for the purposes of this warm-up will be of essay length.

When the short stories are complete, select several students to read their prose aloud to the class, and have the class briefly comment and

discuss them. Open the discussion to the class
to exchange the collective thoughts of the
students on the process of selecting the
elements they believe comprise the satisfactory
achievement of their version of a short story.

Step 2 – Introduction to the Lesson:
Following the warm-up, explain the following
concepts to the class:

   symbolism: A symbol is a person,
place, thing, or event used to stand for
something abstract, such as an idea or emotion,
in a literary work. A symbol represents
something other than itself.

   Discuss the above definition with the
class, and solicit additional definitions from the
students based on their warm-up activity in
order to get their input. Write the additional
definitions or terms on the whiteboard for all to
see. (Using the simple definition above,
teachers should be able to refer to multiple
examples of symbolism found in classic and

contemporary literature in order to direct and extend the class discussion). Students should be directed to use these definitions as guides when participating in the following class activity.

Step 3 – Activity: Following the introduction to the lesson, when each student has formed an opinion about the element of symbolism in fiction prose literature, instruct the class to write a fictionalized short story based on their personal lives. While considering the warm-up session in Step 1 above and the conclusions arrived at in Step 2 above, the class should be instructed to focus its attention on the element of *symbolism* used in fiction prose for this assignment. The short story may be any length, and at the teacher's discretion, may encompass more than one class session.

Teacher's Note: It is very helpful for the teacher to discuss symbolism found in popular movies and television shows. The discussion will make it easier to clarify the concept to the class – and students tend to love this exercise!

Step 4 – Discussion: After the class has completed its short stories, ask for student volunteers to read their prose aloud to the class. Allow for plenty of discussion on the use of *symbolism*. Be sure to discuss the thought patterns generated. Make certain the students in the class provide alternative possibilities for the use of *symbolism* in each story read, and discuss how changing the example of *symbolism* might change the impact on the reader.

Step 5 – Assessment: As a homework assignment, have the students select a significant passage or scene from a short story of their choice, which passage demonstrates the use of *symbolism*. Ask them to create an artistic piece demonstrating the passage or scene they have selected. The artwork may be a drawing, painting, musical composition, or any creative expression of choice, such as a mask, a collage of facial expressions, or newspaper clippings.

They should be prepared to discuss their selection, the reason for the selection, and the resultant artwork in the next class. Teachers will be able to recognize how the class has understood the concept of *symbolism* by viewing the artistic expressions of the students, and paying attention to the reasoning set forth in the student discussions surrounding their art production.

Elements of Fiction: Tone & Mood
(One-Two 45-Minute Class Sessions)

Objective: This exercise is designed to allow students to examine and distinguish two of the major elements of fiction prose. Students will have an opportunity to understand the connection between *tone* and *mood* found in prose literature and contemporary American society, and to focus on both elements of fiction literature when writing their own prose selections.

Step 1 – Warm-up: In this exercise, students are asked to write a short story on a topic of their choice. They should consider ordinary, everyday persons, places, things, or events in their lives as the subject matter of their stories. Due to the time constraints, the short stories written for the purposes of this warm-up will be of essay length.

When the short stories are complete, select several students to read their prose aloud to the class, and have the class briefly comment and discuss them. Open the discussion to the class to exchange the collective thoughts of the students on the process of selecting the elements they believe comprise the satisfactory achievement of their version of a short story.

Step 2 – Introduction to the Lesson:
Following the warm-up, explain the following concepts to the class:

short story: A short story is the telling of a happening or a series of events. It is also a narrative designed to interest, amuse, or inform the reader.

tone: Refers to an author's attitude toward the subject, characters, or reader.

mood: Refers to the atmosphere or feeling conveyed by a literary work.

Discuss the above definitions with the class, and solicit additional definitions from the students based on their warm-up activity in order to get their input. Write the additional definitions or terms on the whiteboard for all to see. (Using the simple definitions above, teachers should be able to refer to multiple examples of tone and mood found in classic and contemporary literature in order to direct and extend the class discussion). Students should be directed to use these definitions as guides when participating in the following class activity.

Step 3 – Activity: Following the introduction to the lesson, when each student has formed an opinion about the elements of tone and mood in fiction prose literature, instruct the class to write a fictionalized short story based on their personal lives. While considering the warm-up session in Step 1 above and the conclusions arrived at in Step 2 above, the class should be instructed to focus its attention on the elements of *tone* and *mood* used in fiction prose for this assignment. The short story may be any length, and at the teacher's discretion, may encompass more than one class session.

Teacher's Note: It is very helpful for the teacher to discuss tone and mood found in popular movies and television shows. The discussion will make it easier to clarify the concept to the class – and students tend to love this exercise!

Step 4 – Discussion: After the class has completed its short stories, ask for student volunteers to read their prose aloud to the class. Allow for plenty of discussion on the use of *tone* and *mood*. Be sure to discuss the thought patterns generated. Make certain the students in the class provide alternative possibilities for the use of *tone* and *mood* in each story read, and discuss how changing the examples of *tone* and *mood* might change the impact on the reader.

Step 5 – Assessment: As a homework assignment, have the students select a significant passage or scene from a short story of their choice, which passage demonstrates the uses of *tone* and *mood*. Ask them to create an artistic piece demonstrating the passage or scene they have selected. The artwork may be a drawing, painting, musical composition, or any creative expression of choice, such as a mask, a collage of facial expressions, or newspaper clippings.

They should be prepared to discuss their selection, the reason for the selection, and the resultant artwork in the next class. Teachers will be able to recognize how the class has understood the concepts of *tone* and *mood* by viewing the artistic expressions of the students, and paying attention to the reasoning set forth in the student discussions surrounding their art production.

Short Story Elements: Flashback
(One-Two 45-Minute Class Sessions)

Objective: This exercise is designed to allow students to examine one of the major elements of a short story. Students will have an opportunity to understand the connection between *flashback* found in classic prose literature and contemporary American society, and to focus on *flashback* when writing their own prose selections.

Step 1 – Warm-up: In this exercise, students are asked to write a short story on a topic of their choice. They should consider ordinary, everyday happenings in their lives as the subject matter of their stories. Due to the time constraints, the short stories written for the purposes of this warm-up will be of essay length.

When the short stories are complete, select several students to read their prose aloud to the class, and have the class briefly comment and

discuss them. Open the discussion to the class to exchange the collective thoughts of the students on the process of selecting the elements they believe comprise the satisfactory achievement of their version of a short story.

Step 2 – Introduction to the Lesson:
Following the warm-up, explain the following concepts to the class:

short story: A short story is the telling of a happening or a series of events. It is also a narrative designed to interest, amuse, or inform the reader.

flashback: A flashback is an interruption in the narrative to show something that happened before that time. A character in the present may think back to a time in the past, or may relate a past event to another character. Information in a flashback can help to explain actions or events in the present.

Discuss the above definitions and concepts with the class, and solicit additional definitions from the students based on their warm-up activity in order to get their input. Write the additional definitions or terms on the whiteboard for all to see. Students should be directed to use these definitions as guides when participating in the following class activity.

Step 3 – Activity: Following the introduction to the lesson, when each student has formed an opinion about the elements of a short story, instruct the class to write a fictionalized short story based on their personal lives. While considering the warm-up session in Step 1 above and the conclusions arrived at in Step 2 above, the class should be instructed to focus its attention on the short story element of *flashback* for this assignment. The short story may be any length, and at the teacher's discretion, may encompass more than one class session.

Teacher's Note: It is very helpful for the teacher to discuss *flashback* found in popular movies and television shows. The discussion will make it easier to clarify the concept to the class – and students tend to love this exercise!

Step 4 – Discussion: After the class has completed its short stories, ask for student volunteers to read their prose aloud to the class. Allow for plenty of discussion on the treatment of *flashback*. Be sure to discuss the thought patterns generated. Make certain the students in the class provide alternative conflicts for each story, and discuss how changing the *flashback* might change the outcome of the short story and its impact on the reader.

Step 5 – Assessment: As a homework assignment, have the students select a significant passage or scene containing a *flashback* from a short story of their choice. Ask them to create an artistic piece demonstrating the passage or scene they have selected. The artwork may be a drawing, painting, musical composition, or any creative expression of choice.

They should be prepared to discuss their selection, the reason for the selection, and the resultant artwork in the next class. Teachers will be able to recognize how the class has understood the concept of *flashback* by viewing the artistic expressions of the students, and paying attention to the reasoning set forth in the student discussions surrounding their art production.

Short Story Elements: Foreshadowing (One-Two 45-Minute Class Sessions)

Objective: This exercise is designed to allow students to examine one of the major elements of a short story. Students will have an opportunity to understand the connection between *foreshadowing* found in classic prose literature and contemporary American society, and to focus on *foreshadowing* when writing their own prose selections.

Step 1 – Warm-up: In this exercise, students are asked to write a short story on a topic of their choice. They should consider ordinary, everyday happenings in their lives as the subject matter of their stories. Due to the time constraints, the short stories written for the purposes of this warm-up will be of essay length.

When the short stories are complete, select several students to read their prose aloud to the class, and have the class briefly comment and

discuss them. Open the discussion to the class to exchange the collective thoughts of the students on the process of selecting the elements they believe comprise the satisfactory achievement of their version of a short story.

Step 2 – Introduction to the Lesson:
Following the warm-up, explain the following concepts to the class:

short story: A short story is the telling of a happening or a series of events. It is also a narrative designed to interest, amuse, or inform the reader.

foreshadowing: Foreshadowing provides hints or clues early in a story that anticipate what is to come. Foreshadowing increases suspense, contributes to mood, and makes the ending seem believable.

Discuss the above definitions and concepts with the class, and solicit additional definitions from the students based on their warm-up activity in order to get their input. Write the additional definitions or terms on the whiteboard for all to see. Students should be directed to use these definitions as guides when participating in the following class activity.

Step 3 – Activity: Following the introduction to the lesson, when each student has formed an opinion about the elements of a short story, instruct the class to write a fictionalized short story based on their personal lives. While considering the warm-up session in Step 1 above and the conclusions arrived at in Step 2 above, the class should be instructed to focus its attention on the short story element of *foreshadowing* for this assignment. The short story may be any length, and at the teacher's discretion, may encompass more than one class session.

Teacher's Note: It is very helpful for the teacher to discuss *foreshadowing* found in popular movies and television shows. The discussion will make it easier to clarify the concept to the class – and students tend to love this exercise!

Step 4 – Discussion: After the class has completed its short stories, ask for student volunteers to read their prose aloud to the class. Allow for plenty of discussion on the treatment of *foreshadowing*. Be sure to discuss the thought patterns generated. Make certain the students in the class provide alternative conflicts for each story, and discuss how changing the *foreshadowing* might change the outcome of the short story and its impact on the reader.

Step 5 – Assessment: As a homework assignment, have the students select a significant passage or scene containing *foreshadowing* from a short story of their choice. Ask them to create an artistic piece demonstrating the passage or scene they have selected. The artwork may be a drawing, painting, musical composition, or any creative expression of choice.

They should be prepared to discuss their selection, the reason for the selection, and the resultant artwork in the next class. Teachers will be able to recognize how the class has understood the concept of *foreshadowing* by viewing the artistic expressions of the students, and paying attention to the reasoning set forth in the student discussions surrounding their art production.

Drama

Acts & Scenes
(Two 45-Minute Class Sessions)

Objective: This exercise is designed to allow students to examine two of the major elements of drama. Students will have an opportunity to understand the structure and content of a dramatic work, to identify the elements of drama considered in a critique of a play, and to focus on *acts* and *scenes* when writing their own dramatic presentations.

Step 1 – Warm-up: In this exercise, students are asked to write a very brief one-act play on a topic of their choice. They should consider ordinary, everyday happenings in their lives as the subject matter of their dramatic work. Due to the time constraints, the warm-up should be limited to 20-25 minutes, although this lesson may be extended to cover several 45-minute class sessions.

When the class plays are complete, select several students to read their drama aloud to the class, and have the class briefly comment and discuss them. Open the discussion to the class to exchange the collective thoughts of the students on the process of selecting the elements they believe comprise the satisfactory achievement of their version of a short play.

Step 2 – Introduction to the Lesson:
Following the warm-up, explain the following literary elements to the class:

drama: A prose or verse composition that is intended for representation by actors impersonating the characters and performing the dialogue and action.

acts: The major divisions in a dramatic work.

scenes: Smaller divisions within an act.

Either time, place, or both may change with each act and scene.

Step 3 – Activity: Ask students to exchange the plays they have written in the warm-up exercise with other class members. Ask the class members receiving the original plays to re-write them, this time breaking down the play into several short dramatic scenes. Be certain the students understand that they may add material and change the play drastically in order to complete this exercise.

Teacher's Note: This exercise is particularly effective because students *learn by doing*. Once given an opportunity to read dramatic works in future lessons as part of the general high school curriculum, identifying the elements of *acts* and *scenes* in drama becomes automatic.

Step 4 – Discussion: When the class has completed the revised plays, select several students to read their works aloud, and discuss them openly. Be certain to point out the designated scenes appearing in each act, and relate the significance of each scene to the overall meaning of the plays written.

Step 5 – Assessment: As a homework assignment, have the students select a one-act play of their choice from their textbooks or the internet, and tell them to be prepared to read the selected plays aloud in class. Students should be able to point out the various dramatic scenes in the plays they choose, and explain how they help readers understand the meaning of each play.

Cast of Characters
(Two 45-Minute Class Sessions)

Objective: This exercise is designed to allow students to examine one of the major elements of drama. Students will have an opportunity to understand the structure and content of a dramatic work, to identify the elements of drama considered in a critique of a play, and to focus on the *cast of characters* when writing their own dramatic presentations.

Step 1 – Warm-up: In this exercise, students are asked to write a very brief one-act play on a topic of their choice, using only two characters. They should consider ordinary, everyday happenings in their lives as the subject matter of their dramatic work. Due to the time constraints, the warm-up should be limited to 20-25 minutes, although this lesson may be extended to cover several 45-minute class sessions.

When the class plays are complete, select several students to read their drama aloud to the class, and have the class briefly comment and discuss them. Open the discussion to the class to exchange the collective thoughts of the students on the process of selecting the elements they believe comprise the satisfactory achievement of their version of a short play.

Step 2 – Introduction to the Lesson:
Following the warm-up, explain the following literary elements to the class:

drama: A prose or verse composition that is intended for representation by actors impersonating the characters and performing the dialogue and action.

cast of characters: A list that tells who is in the play. The list may also describe the characters.

Step 3 – Activity: Ask students to exchange the plays they have written in the warm-up exercise with other class members. Ask the class members receiving the original plays to re-write them, this time adding one character to the plot. Be certain the students understand that they may add material and change the play drastically in order to complete this exercise. The re-written play should include a cast of characters, which describes the three characters in the play.

Teacher's Note: This exercise is particularly effective because students *learn by doing*. Once given an opportunity to read dramatic works in future lessons as part of the general high school curriculum, focus on the *cast of characters* and identifying the individual characters and their respective roles in drama becomes automatic.

Step 4 – Discussion: When the class has completed the revised plays, select several students to read their works aloud, and discuss them openly. Be certain to point out the characters appearing in each act, and relate the significance of each scene to the overall meaning of the plays written. The developed characters should be consistent with their descriptions in the *cast of characters*.

Step 5 – Assessment: As a homework assignment, have the students select a one-act play of their choice from their textbooks or the internet, and tell them to be prepared to read the selected plays aloud in class. Students should be able to point out the various characters in the plays they choose, and their significance. They should be prepared to explain how understanding the characters helps readers understand the meaning of each play.

Dialogue
(Two 45-Minute Class Sessions)

Objective: This exercise is designed to allow students to examine one of the major elements of drama. Students will have an opportunity to understand the structure and content of a dramatic work, to identify the elements of drama considered in a critique of a play, and to focus on the concept of *dialogue* when writing their own dramatic presentations.

Step 1 – Warm-up: In this exercise, students are asked to write a very brief one-scene play on a topic of their choice, using only two characters. They should consider ordinary, everyday happenings in their lives as the subject matter of their dramatic work. Due to the time constraints, the warm-up should be limited to 20-25 minutes, although this lesson may be extended to cover several 45-minute class sessions.

When the class plays are complete, select several students to read their drama aloud to the class, and have the class briefly comment and discuss them. Open the discussion to the class to exchange the collective thoughts of the students on the process of selecting the elements they believe comprise the satisfactory achievement of their version of a short play scene.

Step 2 – Introduction to the Lesson:
Following the warm-up, explain the following literary elements to the class:

drama: A prose or verse composition that is intended for representation by actors impersonating the characters and performing the dialogue and action.

dialogue: Dialogue is the conversation among characters in a play. Analyzing dialogue can help students understand the characters, track the events of the plot, and discover clues to the theme.

speech tags: Indicate the speaker of dialogue in a play.

stage directions: Indicate any action the speaker is to perform.

Step 3 – Activity: Ask students to exchange the play scenes they have written in the warm-up exercise with other class members. Ask the class members receiving the original scenes to re-write them, this time adding more dialogue. Be certain the students understand that they may add material and change the scene drastically in order to complete this exercise. The re-written scene should include new dialogue that adds a different dimension and perhaps alters the meaning, theme, or outcome of the original scene.

Teacher's Note: This exercise is particularly effective because students *learn by doing*. Once given an opportunity to read dramatic works in future lessons as part of the general high school curriculum, focus on the *dialogue* and identifying the individual characters and their respective roles in drama becomes automatic.

Step 4 – Discussion: When the class has completed the revised scenes, select several students to read their works aloud, and discuss them openly. Be certain to point out the characters appearing in each scene, and relate the significance of the dialogue to the overall meaning of the scenes written. The developed characters should be identifiable through their *dialogue.*

Step 5 – Assessment: As a homework assignment, have the students select a one-act play of their choice from their textbooks or the internet, and tell them to be prepared to read the selected plays aloud in class. Students should be able to point out the various characters in the plays they choose, and comment on the dialogue each character uses. They should be prepared to explain how understanding the dialogue helps readers understand the meaning of each play.

Theme
(Two 45-Minute Class Sessions)

Objective: This exercise is designed to allow students to examine one of the major elements of drama. Students will have an opportunity to understand the structure and content of a dramatic work, to identify the elements of drama considered in a critique of a play, and to focus on the concept of *theme* when writing their own dramatic presentations.

Step 1 – Warm-up: In this exercise, students are asked to write a very brief one-scene play on a topic of their choice, using only two characters. They should consider ordinary, everyday happenings in their lives as the subject matter of their dramatic work. Due to the time constraints, the warm-up should be limited to 20-25 minutes, although this lesson may be extended to cover several 45-minute class sessions.

When the class plays are complete, select several students to read their drama aloud to the class, and have the class briefly comment and discuss them. Open the discussion to the class to exchange the collective thoughts of the students on the process of selecting the elements they believe comprise the satisfactory achievement of their version of a short play scene.

Step 2 – Introduction to the Lesson:
Following the warm-up, explain the following literary elements to the class:

drama: A prose or verse composition that is intended for representation by actors impersonating the characters and performing the dialogue and action.

theme: A statement about life around which the playwright builds the play.

Step 3 – Activity: Ask students to exchange the plays they have written in the warm-up exercise with other class members. Ask the class members receiving the original plays to re-write them, this time changing the themes. Be certain the students understand that they may add material and change the scene drastically in order to complete this exercise. The re-written play should include at least one new *theme* that adds a different dimension and perhaps alters the meaning or outcome of the original play.

Teacher's Note: This exercise is particularly effective because students *learn by doing*. Once given an opportunity to read dramatic works in future lessons as part of the general high school curriculum, focus on the *theme* in drama becomes automatic.

Step 4 – Discussion: When the class has completed the revised plays, select several students to read their works aloud, and discuss them openly. Be certain to point out the themes appearing in each play, and relate the significance of the themes to the overall meaning of the plays written. The developed themes should be clearly identifiable through the class discussions.

Step 5 – Assessment: As a homework assignment, have the students select a one-act play of their choice from their textbooks or the internet, and tell them to be prepared to read the selected plays aloud in class. Students should be able to point out the various themes in the plays they choose, and comment on each theme. They should be prepared to explain how understanding the theme helps readers understand the meaning of each play.

Pantomime: Actions
(Two 45-Minute Class Sessions)

Objective: This exercise is designed to allow students to experience some of the major elements of drama. Students will have an opportunity to understand the unwritten components of a dramatic work, to identify the elements of drama considered in a critique of a play, and to focus on the concept of *acting* when considering dramatic presentations.

Step 1 – Warm-up: In this exercise, students are asked to work in pairs, or in groups of no larger than three actors. Students must first discuss among themselves and compile a list of topics of their choice for a two or three character pantomime presentation. They should consider ordinary, everyday happenings in their lives as the subject matter of their dramatic pantomime presentation. The list of *action* topics should include at least ten items, such as visiting the doctor's office or mailing a letter.

When the group lists are complete, each group should continue their discussions amongst themselves, exchanging their collective thoughts on how they will present the action topic, in pantomime, by means of a short play scene.

Step 2 – Introduction to the Lesson:
Following the warm-up, explain the following concepts to the class:

acting: the performance of a part or role in a drama.

pantomime: the art of using movement and facial expressions rather than primarily the spoken word to communicate dramatic ideas and concepts to an audience.

Step 3 – Activity: Ask students in each group formed in the warm-up session to prepare a pantomime presentation from the lists compiled during the warm-up exercise. Ask each group to act out one subject selected from their topic lists. Be certain the students understand that they may NOT add props of any kind in order to complete this exercise. The students in each group will stand in front of the classroom and attempt to get the other class members to guess the action subject they have selected. Two or three minutes would be perfect for a time limitation for each pantomime play.

Teacher's Note: This exercise is particularly effective because students *learn by doing*. Once given an opportunity to act out dramatic parts, students understand the playwright's dilemma in selecting the right language for a play, coupled with the playwright's vision for stage directing in order to *get the message across* to an audience.

Step 4 – Discussion: When the class has completed several of the pantomime presentations, discuss them openly. Be certain to point out the dramatic elements used in each performance to convey the particular action topic presented.

Step 5 – Assessment: As a homework assignment, have the students prepare the dialogue for short, WRITTEN, one-act plays based on their respective pantomime presentations. Tell them to be prepared to act out the selected plays aloud in class using the dialogue. Students should be prepared to compare and comment upon the pantomime and verbal presentations.

Pantomime: The USA
(Two 45-Minute Class Sessions)

Objective: This exercise is designed to allow students to experience some of the major elements of drama. Students will have an opportunity to understand the unwritten components of a dramatic work, to identify the elements of drama considered in a critique of a play, and to focus on the concept of *acting* when considering dramatic presentations.

Step 1 – Warm-up: In this exercise, students are asked to work in pairs, or in groups of no larger than three actors. Students must first discuss among themselves and compile a list of selected states in the USA as topics for a two or three character pantomime presentation. They should consider states that would be easy to act out, such as Hawaii (hula dancing) or Alaska (cold) as the subject matter of their dramatic pantomime presentation. The list of states of the union should include at least ten items, along with some of the characteristics of each of the states selected.

When the group lists are complete, each group should continue their discussions among themselves, exchanging their collective thoughts on how they will present the selected state, in pantomime, by means of a short play scene.

Step 2 – Introduction to the Lesson:
Following the warm-up, explain the following concepts to the class:

acting: the performance of a part or role in a drama.

pantomime: the art of using movement and facial expressions rather than primarily the spoken word to communicate dramatic ideas and concepts to an audience.

Step 3 – Activity: Ask students in each group formed in the warm-up session to prepare a pantomime presentation from the lists of states compiled during the warm-up exercise. Ask each group to act out one subject selected from their lists of states. Be certain the students understand that they may NOT add props of any kind in order to complete this exercise. The students in each group will stand in front of the classroom and attempt to get the other class members to guess the states they have selected as subjects. Two or three minutes would be perfect for a time limitation for each pantomime play.

Teacher's Note: This exercise is particularly effective because students *learn by doing*. Once given an opportunity to act out dramatic parts, students understand the playwright's dilemma in selecting the right language for a play, coupled with the playwright's vision for stage directing in order to *get the message across* to an audience.

Step 4 – Discussion: When the class has completed several of the pantomime presentations, discuss them openly. Be certain to point out the dramatic elements used in each performance to convey the particular characteristics of the state presented.

Step 5 – Assessment: As a homework assignment, have the students prepare the dialogue for short, WRITTEN, one-act plays based on their respective pantomime presentations. Tell them to be prepared to act out the selected plays aloud in class using the dialogue, but must NOT mention the name of the selected state in the dialogue. Students should be prepared to compare and comment upon the pantomime and verbal presentations.

Pantomime: Favorite TV Shows
(Two 45-Minute Class Sessions)

Objective: This exercise is designed to allow students to experience some of the major elements of drama. Students will have an opportunity to understand the unwritten components of a dramatic work, to identify the elements of drama considered in a critique of a play, and to focus on the concept of *acting* when considering dramatic presentations.

Step 1 – Warm-up: In this exercise, students are asked to work in pairs, or in groups of no larger than three actors. Students must first discuss among themselves and compile a list of topics of their choice for a two or three character pantomime presentation. They should consider appropriate, non-offensive television shows as the subject matter of their dramatic pantomime presentation. The list of television shows should include at least ten items, along with a description of each show for teacher approval.

When the group lists are complete, each group should continue their discussions among themselves, exchanging their collective thoughts on how they will present the TV show, in pantomime, by means of a short play scene.

Step 2 – Introduction to the Lesson:
Following the warm-up, explain the following concepts to the class:

acting: the performance of a part or role in a drama.

pantomime: the art of using movement and facial expressions rather than primarily the spoken word to communicate dramatic ideas and concepts to an audience.

Step 3 – Activity: Ask students in each group formed in the warm-up session to prepare a pantomime presentation from the lists compiled during the warm-up exercise. Ask each group to act out one television show selected from their warm-up lists. Be certain the students understand that they may NOT add props of any kind in order to complete this exercise. The students in each group will stand in front of the classroom and attempt to get the other class members to guess the names of the television shows they have selected. Two or three minutes would be perfect for a time limitation for each pantomime play.

Teacher's Note: This exercise is particularly effective because students *learn by doing*. Once given an opportunity to act out dramatic parts, students understand the playwright's dilemma in selecting the right language for a play, coupled with the playwright's vision for stage directing in order to *get the message across* to an audience.

Step 4 – Discussion: When the class has completed several of the pantomime presentations, discuss them openly. Be certain to point out the dramatic elements used in each performance to convey the particular action topic presented.

Step 5 – Assessment: As a homework assignment, have the students prepare the dialogue for short, WRITTEN, one-act plays based on their respective pantomime presentations. Tell them to be prepared to act out the selected plays aloud in class using the dialogue, but must NOT mention the name of the show or any character names. Students should be prepared to compare and comment upon the pantomime and verbal presentations.

Pantomime: Favorite Songs
(Two 45-Minute Class Sessions)

Objective: This exercise is designed to allow students to experience some of the major elements of drama. Students will have an opportunity to understand the unwritten components of a dramatic work, to identify the elements of drama considered in a critique of a play, and to focus on the concept of *acting* when considering dramatic presentations.

Step 1 – Warm-up: In this exercise, students are asked to work in pairs, or in groups of no larger than three actors. Students must first discuss among themselves and compile a list of topics of their choice for a two or three character pantomime presentation. They should consider appropriate, non-offensive popular songs as the subject matter of their dramatic pantomime presentation. The list of popular songs should include at least ten items, along with a description of each show for teacher approval.

When the group lists are complete, each group should continue their discussions among themselves, exchanging their collective thoughts on how they will present the chosen songs, in pantomime, by means of a short play scene.

Step 2 – Introduction to the Lesson: Following the warm-up, explain the following concepts to the class:

acting: the performance of a part or role in a drama.

pantomime: the art of using movement and facial expressions rather than primarily the spoken word to communicate dramatic ideas and concepts to an audience.

Step 3 – Activity: Ask students in each group formed in the warm-up session to prepare a pantomime presentation from the lists compiled during the warm-up exercise. Ask each group to act out one popular selected from their warm-up lists. Be certain the students understand that they may NOT add props of any kind in order to complete this exercise. The students in each group will stand in front of the classroom and attempt to get the other class members to guess the names of the popular songs they have selected. Two or three minutes would be perfect for a time limitation for each pantomime play.

Teacher's Note: This exercise is particularly effective because students *learn by doing*. Once given an opportunity to act out dramatic parts, students understand the playwright's dilemma in selecting the right language for a play, coupled with the playwright's vision for stage directing in order to *get the message across* to an audience.

Step 4 – Discussion: When the class has completed several of the pantomime presentations, discuss them openly. Be certain to point out the dramatic elements used in each performance to convey the particular action topic presented.

Step 5 – Assessment: As a homework assignment, have the students prepare the dialogue for short, WRITTEN, one-act plays based on their respective pantomime presentations. Tell them to be prepared to act out the selected plays aloud in class using the dialogue, but must NOT mention the name of the popular songs or their authors/singers. Students should be prepared to compare and comment upon the pantomime and verbal presentations.

Pantomime: Favorite Books
(Two 45-Minute Class Sessions)

Objective: This exercise is designed to allow students to experience some of the major elements of drama. Students will have an opportunity to understand the unwritten components of a dramatic work, to identify the elements of drama considered in a critique of a play, and to focus on the concept of *acting* when considering dramatic presentations.

Step 1 – Warm-up: In this exercise, students are asked to work in pairs, or in groups of no larger than three actors. Students must first discuss among themselves and compile a list of topics of their choice for a two or three character pantomime presentation. They should consider appropriate, non-offensive books or literary works, such as famous short stories, as the subject matter of their dramatic pantomime presentation. The list of books or literary works should include at least ten items, along with a description of each book for teacher approval.

When the group lists are complete, each group should continue their discussions amongst themselves, exchanging their collective thoughts on how they will present the books or literary works, in pantomime, by means of a short play scene.

Step 2 – Introduction to the Lesson:
Following the warm-up, explain the following concepts to the class:

acting: the performance of a part or role in a drama.

pantomime: the art of using movement and facial expressions rather than primarily the spoken word to communicate dramatic ideas and concepts to an audience.

Step 3 – Activity: Ask students in each group formed in the warm-up session to prepare a pantomime presentation from the lists compiled during the warm-up exercise. Ask each group to act out one books or literary work selected from their warm-up lists. Be certain the students understand that they may NOT add props of any kind in order to complete this exercise. The students in each group will stand in front of the classroom and attempt to get the other class members to guess the names of the books or literary works they have selected. Two or three minutes would be perfect for a time limitation for each pantomime play.

Teacher's Note: This exercise is particularly effective because students *learn by doing*. Once given an opportunity to act out dramatic parts, students understand the playwright's dilemma in selecting the right language for a play, coupled with the playwright's vision for stage directing in order to *get the message across* to an audience.

Step 4 – Discussion: When the class has completed several of the pantomime presentations, discuss them openly. Be certain to point out the dramatic elements used in each performance to convey the particular books or literary works presented.

Step 5 – Assessment: As a homework assignment, have the students prepare the dialogue for short, WRITTEN, one-act plays based on their respective pantomime presentations. Tell them to be prepared to act out the selected plays aloud in class using the dialogue, but must NOT mention the name of the books or literary works, or their authors. Students should be prepared to compare and comment upon the pantomime and verbal presentations.

One-Minute Monologues
(Two 45-Minute Class Sessions)

Objective: This exercise is designed to allow students to examine the concept of *monologue* in drama. Students will have an opportunity to understand the structure and content of a dramatic work, to identify the elements of drama considered in a critique of a play, and to focus on *monologue* when writing their own dramatic presentations, and distinguish monologue from dialogue.

Step 1 – Warm-up: In this exercise, students are asked to write a very brief speech on a topic of their choice. They should consider ordinary, everyday happenings in their lives as the subject matter of their speeches, which will ultimately form the basis of a dramatic work. The speeches must deliver to an audience the emotions, feelings, gripes, or needs of a typical teenager in the twenty-first century. Due to the time constraints, the warm-up should be limited to 20-25 minutes, although this lesson may be extended to cover several 45-minute class sessions.

When the class speeches are complete, select several students to read their productions aloud to the class, and have the class briefly comment on and discuss them. Open the discussion to the class to exchange the collective thoughts of the students on the process of selecting the elements they believe comprise the satisfactory achievement of their speeches, and how each might be converted to a one-act play.

Step 2 – Introduction to the Lesson:
Following the warm-up, explain the following literary elements to the class:

drama: A prose or verse composition that is intended for representation by actors impersonating the characters and performing the dialogue and action.

cast of characters: A list that tells who is in the play. The list may also describe the characters.

dialogue: Dialogue is the conversation among characters in a play. Analyzing dialogue can help students understand the characters, track the events of the plot, and discover clues to the theme.

monologue: A long speech spoken by a character in the presence of others.

Step 3 – Activity: Ask students to exchange the speeches they have written in the warm-up exercise with other class members. Ask the class members receiving the original speeches to re-write them, this time converting the speeches into a single, short dramatic scene. Be certain the students understand that they may add material and change the speeches drastically in order to complete this exercise.

Teacher's Note: This exercise is particularly effective because students *learn by doing.* Once given an opportunity to read dramatic works in future lessons as part of the general high school curriculum, identifying the powerful impact of monologues and soliloquies in drama becomes automatic.

Step 4 – Discussion: When the class has completed the revised plays, select several students to read their works aloud, and discuss them openly. Be certain to point out the dramatic elements appearing in each monologue, and relate the significance of each to the overall meaning of the monologues written.

Step 5 – Assessment: As a homework assignment, have the students select a monologue or one-act play of their choice from their textbooks or the internet, and tell them to be prepared to read the selected plays aloud in class. Students should be able to point out the dramatic impact upon the audience of the monologues they choose, and explain what elements help readers understand the meaning of each presentation.

One-Minute Soliloquies
(Two 45-Minute Class Sessions)

Objective: This exercise is designed to allow students to examine the concept of *soliloquy* in drama. Students will have an opportunity to understand the structure and content of a dramatic work, to identify the elements of drama considered in a critique of a play, and to focus on *soliloquy* when writing their own dramatic presentations, and distinguish soliloquy from monologue.

Step 1 – Warm-up: In this exercise, students are asked to write very brief speeches on a topic of their choice. They should consider ordinary, everyday happenings in their lives as the subject matter of their speeches. The speeches must deliver to an audience the emotions, feelings, gripes, or needs of a typical teenager in the twenty-first century. Due to the time constraints, the warm-up should be limited to 20-25 minutes, although this lesson may be extended to cover several 45-minute class sessions.

When the class speeches are complete, select several students to read their speeches aloud to the class, and have the class briefly comment on and discuss them. Open the discussion to the class to exchange the collective thoughts of the students on the process of selecting the elements they believe comprise the satisfactory achievement of their speeches, and how each might be converted to a one-act play.

Step 2 – Introduction to the Lesson:
Following the warm-up, explain the following literary elements to the class:

drama: A prose or verse composition that is intended for representation by actors impersonating the characters and performing the dialogue and action.

cast of characters: A list that tells who is in the play. The list may also describe the characters.

monologue: a long speech spoken by a character in the presence of others.

soliloquy: a long speech delivered when the speaker is alone.

Step 3 – Activity: Ask students to exchange the speeches they have written in the warm-up exercise with other class members. Ask the class members receiving the original speeches to re-write them, this time converting the speeches into a single, short dramatic scene. Be certain the students understand that they may add material and change the speeches drastically in order to complete this exercise.

Teacher's Note: This exercise is particularly effective because students *learn by doing*. The key to this exercise is to get students to understand that the dramatic scenes they create are supposed to be part of a greater work. Students must understand that a soliloquy is one scene in a play with more than one character, where the speaker is outside the presence of others.

Step 4 – Discussion: When the class has completed the revised plays, select several students to read their works aloud, and discuss them openly. Be certain to point out the dramatic elements appearing in each soliloquy, and relate the significance of each to the overall meaning of the soliloquies written.

Step 5 – Assessment: As a homework assignment, have the students select a soliloquy from a play of their choice from their textbooks or the internet, and tell them to be prepared to read the soliloquies aloud in class. Students should be able to point out the dramatic impact upon the audience of the soliloquies they choose, and explain what elements help readers understand the meaning of each presentation.

One-Act Plays: Single Character
(Two 45-Minute Class Sessions)

Objective: This exercise is designed to allow students to examine several of the major elements of drama. Students will have an opportunity to understand the structure and content of a dramatic work, to identify the elements of drama considered in a critique of a play, and to focus on *acts* and *scenes* and the concepts of *monologue* and *soliloquy* when writing their own dramatic presentations.

Step 1 – Warm-up: In this exercise, students are asked to write a very brief one-act, one-scene play on a topic of their choice. Each play must contain only one character. They should consider ordinary, everyday happenings in their lives as the subject matter of their dramatic work. Due to the time constraints, the warm-up should be limited to 20-25 minutes, although this lesson may be extended to cover several 45-minute class sessions.

When the class plays are complete, select several students to read their drama aloud to the class, and have the class briefly comment and discuss them. Open the discussion to the class to exchange the collective thoughts of the students on the process of selecting the elements they believe comprise the satisfactory achievement of their version of a short play.

Step 2 – Introduction to the Lesson:

Following the warm-up, explain the following literary elements to the class:

acts: The major divisions in a dramatic work.

scenes: Smaller divisions within an act.

monologue: A long speech spoken by a character in the presence of others.

soliloquy: A long speech delivered when the speaker is alone.

Either time, place, or both may change with each act and scene.

Step 3 – Activity: Ask students to exchange the plays they have written in the warm-up exercise with other class members. Ask the class members receiving the original plays to re-write them, this time breaking down the play into several short dramatic scenes. Be certain the students understand that they may add material and change the play drastically in order to complete this exercise.

Teacher's Note: This exercise is particularly effective because students *learn by doing.* Once given an opportunity to read dramatic works in future lessons as part of the general high school curriculum, identifying the elements of *acts, scenes,* and *monologues* in drama becomes automatic. Teachers should point out to the class that the scenes in their plays are monologues, as opposed to soliloquies, because the actors are delivering their thoughts in the presence of others.

Consequently, each scene must be set up properly to allow the audience to believe others are present to hear the delivery in each of the scenes.

Step 4 – Discussion: When the class has completed the revised plays, select several students to read their works aloud, and discuss them openly. Be certain to point out the designated scenes appearing in each act, and relate the significance of each scene to the overall meaning of the plays written.

Step 5 – Assessment: As a homework assignment, have the students select a one-act, one-character play of their choice from their textbooks or the internet, and tell them to be prepared to read the selected plays aloud in class. Students should be able to point out the various dramatic scenes in the plays they choose, and explain how they help readers understand the meaning of each play.

One-Act Plays: Multiple Characters
(Two 45-Minute Class Sessions)

Objective: This exercise is designed to allow students to examine several of the major elements of drama. Students will have an opportunity to understand the structure and content of a dramatic work, to identify the elements of drama considered in a critique of a play, and to focus on *acts* and *scenes* and the concepts of *monologue* and *soliloquy* when writing their own dramatic presentations.

Step 1 – Warm-up: In this exercise, students are asked to write a very brief one-act, one-scene play on a topic of their choice. Each play must contain more than one character. They should consider ordinary, everyday happenings in their lives as the subject matter of their dramatic work. Due to the time constraints, the warm-up should be limited to 20-25 minutes, although this lesson may be extended to cover several 45-minute class sessions.

When the class plays are complete, select several students to read their drama aloud to the class, and have the class briefly comment and discuss them. Open the discussion to the class to exchange the collective thoughts of the students on the process of selecting the elements they believe comprise the satisfactory achievement of their version of a short play.

Step 2 – Introduction to the Lesson:
Following the warm-up, explain the following literary elements to the class:

acts: The major divisions in a dramatic work.

scenes: Smaller divisions within an act.

dialogue: Dialogue is the conversation among characters in a play. Analyzing dialogue can help students understand the characters, track the events of the plot, and discover clues to the theme.

monologue: A long speech spoken by a character in the presence of others.

soliloquy: A long speech delivered when the speaker is alone.

Either time, place, or both may change with each act and scene.

Step 3 – Activity: Ask students to exchange the plays they have written in the warm-up exercise with other class members. Ask the class members receiving the original plays to re-write them, this time breaking down the play into several short dramatic scenes. Be certain the students understand that they may add material and change the play drastically in order to complete this exercise.

Teacher's Note: This exercise is particularly effective because students *learn by doing*. Once given an opportunity to read dramatic works in future lessons as part of the general high school curriculum, identifying the elements of *acts, scenes, dialogue, soliloquies,* and *monologues* in drama becomes automatic. Teachers should point out to the class that the scenes in their plays must include dialogue, as well as at least one monologue and one soliloquy. Scenes containing monologues or soliloquies must be set up properly to allow the audience to believe others are or are not present to hear the delivery in the scenes written.

Step 4 – Discussion: When the class has completed the revised plays, select several students to read their works aloud, and discuss them openly. Be certain to point out the designated scenes appearing in each act, and relate the significance of each scene to the overall meaning of the plays written.

Step 5 – Assessment: As a homework assignment, have the students select a one-act, multiple-character play of their choice from their textbooks or the internet, and tell them to be prepared to read the selected plays aloud in class. Students should be able to point out the various dramatic scenes in the plays they choose, and explain how they help readers understand the meaning of each play.

About the Author

JJ Botta is an author, college professor, and freelance writer in the field of Humanities. He has nine published books on academic subjects to his credit, plus a murder-mystery short story collection, and a memoir. His resumé also contains numerous magazine and online publications on a variety of topics. His most popular works include:

A Writing Safety Net: The Survival Kit For Those Who Have Forgotten – And Those Who Never Learned

Surviving the Journey: A Universal Approach for the Student Critic

Ernest Hemingway's "A Moveable Feast": A Study in the Genre of Memoir

He resides with his wife in St. Augustine, Florida, where he currently teaches Language Arts and Humanities.